dare to be

DEVOTED

Part Two

30 Day Devotional by Natalie Grant and Charlotte Gambill

dare to be

DEVOTED
Part Two

30 Day Devotional

Natalie Grant & *Charlotte Gambill*

www.daretobe.com

We dedicate this book to you, the one holding these pages in your hands and a dream in your heart. We are cheering you on through these words, believing they will help you on your journey to becoming exactly who God has designed you to be. So turn the pages and open your heart. Hold on to hope and be brave with your life. You have got this and God has got you.

—Natalie & Charlotte

A special thanks to Caroline Lusk. Without you, these pages would not have come to life.

—Natalie

CONTENTS

dare to be

d

Truth or Dare? It's one of the oldest questions in the world and somewhat of an odd one. While you can dare to do or be many things, can anyone truly pursue, speak or live truth without a little bit of daring? To seek truth is inherently a risk-taking activity. It unearths answers and reveals things we may not be ready to know or to be known by others.

Yet God doesn't waver when it comes to truth. It's kind of His thing. And He desires for you to seek truth, to know love and to live boldly in light of them both.

A few years ago, we dared you to be a number of things—fearless, yourself, honest. This time around, we're doing the same but asking you to go even deeper. It's not just about daring yourself to reflect on your life. It's about daring you to create a life that's filled with truth and oriented around the passionate pursuit of all things holy, righteous, good and pure.

So when you have to choose between truth or dare, our prayer is that you will dare to pursue truth—emphatically and unequivocally.

Go ahead...we dare you!

Nat and Charl

dare to

LET HIM HAVE THE FIRST WORD

by G

DARE TO *LET HIM HAVE THE FIRST WORD*

Trust God from the bottom of your heart; don't try to figure out everything on your own. Listen for God's voice in everything you do, everywhere you go; he's the one who will keep you on track. Don't assume that you know it all. Run to God! ...But don't, dear friend, resent God's discipline; don't sulk under his loving correction. It's the child he loves that God corrects; a father's delight is behind all this.

Proverbs 3:6-12 (MSG)

Trust manifests in many different ways. We can trust someone with our property. We can demonstrate trust by giving someone a new opportunity or we can trust someone enough to step into a new relationship. Trust, just like faith, has many different levels. We discover these levels the more we are willing to replace our urgency to control everything with trust in He who holds all things. Trust is a journey we have to choose to take. When we first said, "Yes," to God's Lordship of our life, we accepted that we had a need for a Heavenly Father and the journey of His Fathering in our lives began. Trust is the traveling companion we all need in order to move this journey from the starting point into new adventures.

God wants you to invite Him in; not just to provide for and guide you, but to discover a depth of trust that lets Him correct and, at times, discipline you. God is a good Father and each aspect of His Fathering of our lives requires our trust. Often God's correction in our lives seems costly, and works against our own sense of what we feel is just, or even what feels good. One of the areas where this shows up is in the way we communicate, particularly with people who may have been unkind to us, misjudged us or even mistreated us. In these moments of vulnerability, we must learn to trust His way of handling what our own unchecked emotions would often mishandle. Magnifying God's voice first means we allow His words to shape ours; we submit our voice to being changed to sound more like His.

When we talk to God first, it often changes to whom we talk next and the manner in which we conduct the conversation. It's not always easy. Often we just want to say what we feel needs saying. We have an urgency to react or a burning desire to share some news. Conversations are good, sharing can be healthy and voicing concerns or questions is part of the journey. If we want to be healthier rather than hurtful, more hopeful than doubtful, then we have to take it to God first. He is always available. He's a great listener. He doesn't get upset when you're upset. He will never add fuel to a fire that needs putting out. He may not even reply to your question or your concern, but time spent talking with Him will always alter your tone and often diffuse your dilemma. Talk to Him everyday and let Him direct you with what to say next.

DAILY DARE

1. What conversations are you desperate to have, but know your message should first be tempered by your Heavenly Father?

2. Do you find your voice sounds more like His during some seasons than others? Why? Try to determine what it is you're doing when you sound the most like Him.

3. Pray for the patience to hold your tongue even when you're dying to let it loose. Seek His voice, tone and message before you share yours with others.

dare to be

TRANSFORMED

by ng

DARE TO BE *TRANSFORMED*

*Now the Lord is the Spirit, and where the Spirit of the Lord is,
there is freedom. And we all, with unveiled face, beholding the glory
of the Lord, are being transformed into the same image from one degree
of glory to another. For this comes from the Lord who is the Spirit.*

2 Corinthians 3:17-18 (NIV)

On May 7, 1957, Martin Luther King Jr. delivered a keynote address in front of the Lincoln Memorial during the Prayer Pilgrimage for Freedom. It had been three years since the passage of the Civil Rights Act, which legally dissolved the doctrine of "separate but equal."

The act was a good change. A necessary change.

But it wasn't transformational.

King noted that existing social infrastructures of racism still held sway over much of the south. Despite the legislation, most Black people were still denied the right to vote. Without which, one can never truly be free.

"So long as I do not firmly and irrevocably possess the right to vote I do not possess myself. I cannot make up my mind—it is made up for me. I cannot live as a democratic citizen, observing the laws I have helped to enact—I can only submit to the edict of others."

It wasn't enough that a few changes had been made. External change doesn't lead to transformation. Transformation occurs from the inside out—when a willingness to change intersects with surrender.

Romans 12:2 reads:

"Do not be conformed to this world, but be transformed by the renewal of your mind, that by testing you may discern what is the will of God, what is good and acceptable and perfect."

I find it incredibly ironic, exhilarating and absolutely magnificent that these words were written by Paul. Most of us know him as one of the greatest missionaries of all time. His story is even more mind-boggling when you consider the origin.

He was not a preacher's kid. He was not a sympathizer or even a passive observer of the seismic humanitarian shift brought about by Jesus, His disciples and His message of grace, surrender and life. He openly and radically tried to wipe out this movement through whatever means necessary, including murder.

For God to then explicitly choose him to be His greatest mouthpiece, is a testament to not only the power of God to change a life and heart completely; but also to the impact beyond a single individual.

God could have prompted Paul to stop killing Christians or to silence his persecution. But God's not really into surface.

He dug deeper. He took Paul all the way. Because of that transformation, countless millions of people were impacted with the message of the Gospel through Paul's many journeys while he was living and through his words, even unto death.

God doesn't do halfway. He never said to make a few changes...or to do things a little differently than the rest of the world. He commands and creates transformation.

Martin Luther King, Jr. knew that a few new laws were not enough to transform decades of engrained racism and inequality. He knew that this country had to go all in—to give everyone the right to vote in order for true transformation to take place.

So what's holding you back today? Are there areas of your life that you know should be different, but you haven't made the time to or found the energy to address completely?

God wants nothing but the best for His children. That means you! He wants you to have life to the full. But it's all or nothing. You can't be new if you're still holding onto the old.

Now's the time to do it differently. Don't just make a change—make a leap. Fly into the unknown with the only knowledge you'll ever need—God's got you. He sees you. He wants you. If ever there were proof of His radical love for you, look no further than the cross. He didn't go halfway. You weren't meant to either. So be bold. Be different. Be transformed.

DAILY DARE

1. Make a list of the top five things in your life that are preventing you from true transformation. Commit to praying every day for those things. Pray for wisdom, discernment and the courage to let them go.

2. Do one thing every day to step towards the life you want and are meant to live. Call your husband at lunch and tell him you love him. Go for a walk outside and avoid the vending machine. Go to the gym instead of home to a Netflix binge. Do something. Stop standing still.

3. Pray for conviction. Pray that the obstacles in your heart and life demand your utmost attention. Pray that they matter as much to you as they do to the One who created you.

dare to

EMPTY THE TRASH

by G

DARE TO *EMPTY THE TRASH*

Let us run with endurance the race that is set before us,
looking unto Jesus, the author and finisher of our faith,
who for the joy that was set before Him endured the cross.

Hebrews 12:1-2

Every week we have trash collectors come to our home. However, they will only take from us what we remember to put out on the street for collection. If we fail to put the rubbish outside, they won't come inside our home and collect it for us. Nor will they wait for us to remember it's collection time. They don't knock on the door to alert us of the moment we are about to miss. They simply come and take whatever you have bagged up and left for them to take. Uncollected trash can become a real problem. When the contents are left to rot in your home, they become toxic, smelly and leave the surrounding spaces unsanitary.

Do you have some rubbish in your life that should go? Spiritually, we need to be active in placing the things that are no longer purposeful for the future, nor healthy for consumption, into the waste can. Yet that alone is not the complete process. Moving the trash to the can is good, but the can then has to leave the house. You must put the trash in a place where it can be removed and not leave it where it can rot. Put the offense out so that God's grace can remove it; take the bad attitude out and allow forgiveness to collect it. Remove the rotting relationship and the negative thinking. Put it out of your life completely. Remove it from your neighborhood entirely. When yesterday's rubbish remains in your today, it will contaminate the fresh of your future with the stale of the past. Don't be negligent with your rubbish disposal. It may be a task you want to avoid; but it is one you cannot afford to ignore.

Today, stop searching through your trash. Take it out and leave it where it belongs. It's rubbish and it needs to be removed so you can move on.

Your heart is not built to retain and recycle your waste. Your rubbish needs to go away—completely.

One last thing to note—rubbish collection happens on a regular basis on my street. Every week they show up. It's a good schedule and one you should adopt too. A huge clear-out once a year is too heavy and overwhelming. If we don't stay vigilant on our rubbish removal we will begin to suffer from hoarder syndrome.

Our accumulation of toxic thinking, damaging relationships from the past, overflowing piles of unresolved offenses will quickly begin to take over our homes! It will make our space smaller, restrict our movement and even block our entry and access points. It will make our lives harder to share or for others to visit. Ultimately we become less welcoming to any of the new thoughts, opportunities and people God wants to send to our address. You are not called to keep the trash nor hoard the hurt!

So today, be diligent in your daily disciplines of removing rot and letting go of waste. Start embracing the new space your diligence will extend to you.

db

DAILY DARE

1. What are you holding on to right now, despite being aware of its toxicity? Why?

2. Do you have a space at which you can dispose your trash? Is there a friend, family member or counselor who can help you process and eliminate your rubbish?

3. Every week, make a pledge to throw away one thing. Let go of one offense, one habit, one toxic relationship. Whatever your trash may be, create a schedule and process of elimination and pray for the energy and desire to see it through.

dare to be

RELENTLESS

by ng

DARE TO BE *RELENTLESS*

*Do you see what this means—all these pioneers who blazed the way,
all these veterans cheering us on? It means we'd better get on with it.
Strip down, start running—and never quit! No extra spiritual fat,
no parasitic sins. Keep your eyes on Jesus, who both began and finished this
race we're in. Study how he did it. Because he never lost sight of where he
was headed—that exhilarating finish in and with God—he could put up with
anything along the way: Cross, shame, whatever. And now he's there, in the
place of honor, right alongside God. When you find yourselves flagging
in your faith, go over that story again, item by item, that long litany of
hostility he plowed through. That will shoot adrenaline into your souls!*

Hebrews 12:1 (MSG)

It was 1945 and Okinawa was quickly earning its ranking as the bloodiest
theater of World War II. Faced with an invisible, unyielding enemy,
American soldiers braved atrocities and demonstrated a degree of
courage that you and I will hopefully never have to experience first-hand.
Each and every one could teach us a life-altering lesson in perseverance,
camaraderie and bravery. There is one soldier, in particular, whose story
has struck me to the core.

Desmond Doss was, as he called it, a "Conscientious Cooperator." A
deeply devoted Seventh-Day Adventist, he was bound and convicted
that he could never take another life, even in warfare. He had even made
a promise to God, following a terrifying encounter with his father and
uncle, that he would never touch a gun again.

Like most young men at the time, the attack on Pearl Harbor struck
Doss personally and he knew he had to serve his country in battle. So he
enlisted as a combat medic, but refused to bear arms.

His company didn't understand. His commanders and captains thought he was crazy and possibly even dangerous. When they looked at Doss, they saw a skinny kid who wore his religion on his shoulder and would be essentially worthless in combat.

Despite outright brutality and opposition from his fellow soldiers, Doss did not relent his principles or his calling. And when his battalion arrived at Hacksaw Ridge, one of the last strong-holds in the Pacific, he would demonstrate the kind of relentless bravery that only happens in movies.

By himself, Doss carried 75 men from the battlefield, lowered them on a self-made harness down the cliff and gave them a second chance at life. Many of the men who had belittled him were saved by him. And through a night of physical pain and trial that I can only imagine, Doss uttered a prayer that I hope will become part of my daily mantra—"Lord, help me get one more."

If you've seen the movie, Hacksaw Ridge, I'd be stunned if you could make it through without shedding some tears (or several!). The commitment to God, country, brother, ideals and conviction is of a caliber I've rarely, if ever, seen.

Not only was Doss relentless on the battlefield, rescuing soldier after soldier; he was relentless in his beliefs. Regardless of the persecution he received or the battles he had to fight just because of who he was, he never relented or yielded his convictions.

I pray for conviction like that. I want to be the kind of person who can go through the most extreme circumstances and come through singing the praise of my victorious God. I want my faith to be that relentless.

Many days, by the grace of God, it is. But even when my faith seems shaky or my footing unsure, I know that I know that I know that I serve a God who is endlessly relentless. Be it the pursuit of my heart, the unveiling of His compassion or silent answers to prayer, the God that is living inside of me never gives up, never backs down and never lets go.

I think we all know and concede that life can be hard. It hurts sometimes. I think of Paul in prison...or Paul being beaten...or Paul being run out of yet another city and I can't help but wonder how he didn't just throw in the towel. But when I look closer, I see in his story the same that I see in Doss's...the same as in many stories of victory—complete submission to and reliance upon the good and perfect will of God.

Today, as you open one more bill or replay that painful loss over and over, simply mutter the simple prayer — "Lord, help me get one more. One more day. One more dollar. One more chance. One more time."

He will listen and He will answer in His time and in His own way. His love is relentless. And when you let Him in, you can be too.

DAILY DARE

1. Focus your intentions. Identify your convictions and your goals. Know what it is you are aiming for and who it is that you want to be.

2. Go get it. If you have to traverse rocky territory, unknown dangers or treacherous land, put on your helmet and dare to go.

3. Pray without ceasing. Pray for Him to help you get just one more. His power and sustenance never relent or run out. Pray for Him to pour His strength, resolve and courage into you and then go out there and get one more. And then another. And then another.

dare to

OVERCOME MISUNDERSTANDINGS

by G

DARE TO *OVERCOME MISUNDERSTANDINGS*

But the Lord was with Joseph and showed him mercy, and He gave him favor in the sight of the keeper of the prison. And the keeper of the prison committed to Joseph's hand all the prisoners who were in the prison; whatever they did there, it was his doing. The keeper of the prison did not look into anything that was under Joseph's authority, because the Lord was with him; and whatever he did, the Lord made it prosper.

Genesis 29:21-23

Have you ever felt misunderstood? Have your words been taken out of context or your actions misinterpreted? Maybe what you meant to be helpful, someone else read as hurtful. Perhaps something you were anticipating was completely derailed because others misunderstood circumstances or needs.

Misunderstandings are frequent occurrences on this journey through life, therefore we need to know how to neutralize the power they hold or we will waste years trying to prove what doesn't need to be proven. Misunderstanding creates a minefield of dangers; it is a breeding ground for wrong assumptions and a holding pattern in which hurts keep circling. Misunderstandings separate friends, tear people from communities, replace truth with lies and divide what God wants to unite. The phantom menace of misunderstanding is more sinister than we often realize. It is a perpetrator we must become better identifying and responding to.

Misunderstanding can become a set of unspoken feelings that create an ocean of confusion and eventually strand people on an island called isolation. Today, what misunderstanding do you need to stop feeding? We all have questions unanswered and offenses that want to fester. Don't allow the misunderstanding to change the places you should be and the life you are called to fulfill.

When Joseph was thrown in prison for something he did not even do, he had to deal not only with the false accusations, but the misunderstanding surrounding his own integrity and actions. Where he had been entrusted, he was now being judged for being untrustworthy. Where once his hands had been perceived as safe, he was accused of being one whose hands had caused harm. Joseph went to prison convicted for a crime he didn't commit and misunderstood by people who he had only ever tried to help. Yet Joseph did not sit in prison trying to tell everyone how misunderstood he was. Instead, he closed the gap and let his life tell its own story. He silenced the misunderstanding with his upstanding character; he chose not to let his erroneous conviction create a further rift between himself and Pharaoh. When Pharaoh would inquire after Joseph, the report he received spoke not of a man that was bitter, but a young man who was taking his misunderstanding and using it to become better. These choices insured that when the time was right, Joseph could re-enter the world he was destined to help lead.

Often we allow the space misunderstanding creates to be so wide, it prevents us from ever getting back to the place where God had planned for us to play our part.

Don't uproot because of misunderstanding. It's not worth it. Rather, dig deeper. We are all imperfect people trying to figure out how to get along— how to close the gap. Don't allow the menace called misunderstanding to cause you to miss out on any places or people where your future may be calling.

DAILY DARE

1. In what areas of your life do you feel misunderstood?

2. Can you recall a time when you misunderstood someone else?

3. Close the gap. Start with one person and an honest conversation. The next week, focus on someone else. Be intentional about repairing and preventing the havoc misunderstanding can wreak.

dare to be

UNSTUCK

by ng

DARE TO BE *UNSTUCK*

I have come that they may have life and have it to the full.

John 10:10 (NIV)

Have you ever felt like you're sprinting on the treadmill of life and going absolutely nowhere? When you think of your future, do you envision something worth anticipating or just the same old same old?

If you said yes to either, you might be stuck. What's more, you might not even realize it!

I know in my own life, some ruts are easier to identify than others. My girls would likely agree with me were I to admit that I get in a kitchen rut. Somehow, come dinner-time or lunch-time, my creativity takes a break and I end up making the same things over and over again. It's not that the food is unhealthy or unpleasant; it's simply monotonous. And when I think about finding new recipes, making time to shop for unfamiliar ingredients or use unfamiliar, different techniques or kitchen tools, the task just seems daunting. It's hard to reconcile drumming up enough energy to become a maestro at the stove.

There is, however, an upside to this personal realization...take-out!

Other realizations of our personal patterns and behaviors, however, can be significantly more daunting. If we are in a relationship that is going nowhere, a professional situation that seems to have stalled or any other trial that feels like a stalemate, it's time to ask some hard questions, conduct some honest self-evaluation and hit our knees.

Jesus doesn't want us to live in a rut. In John, we read that He came so that our lives would be full! He did not come so that they would be mundane, safe, stale or even comfortable. He came so that we could live in the fullness of His love.

I find the story of Jesus' first and last appearances to the disciples on the shore of the Sea of Galilee such a beautiful representation of the way in which Jesus calls us to live. You may recall that Peter's first interaction with Jesus was on the Sea of Galilee. Jesus, a complete stranger, advises Peter, the seasoned fishermen, to cast his nets on the other side.

I can just hear the inner dialogue!

"Who is this guy and who is he to advise me about fishing?"

Long story short, Peter gives the advice a go, puts his nets on the other side and caught so many fish, the nets began to break!

I can imagine it was pretty chaotic to haul in that kind of a catch. This rich reward was a messy one, but one beyond what Peter could have ever imagined.

I don't think it's inconsequential that when Jesus appears to His disciples after the crucifixion and resurrection that nearly the identical scenario plays out. Peter and the others are fishing, have no luck and then this guy from the beach tells them to try something new.

That was the moment they knew who was calling to them.

They recognized their risen Savior by His encouragement to break out of an unproductive rut and the corresponding abundant results. They knew Jesus by His guidance that led to results bigger than they had dreamed. They knew Jesus by His bold suggestion to do something new; to get unstuck.

Jesus wants the same for you and for me. He doesn't want us to run on a treadmill. He wants us to scale a mountain! He doesn't want us to stay safe in a foxhole, but to boldly run the gauntlet. He doesn't want our faith or our relationships or our calling to grow tired and stale. Rather, He desires to breathe new life into them everyday.

If you feel like you're moving ahead at 0 MPH, perhaps it's time to do some sincere evaluation. Ask yourself the hard questions and be bold enough to seek and profess the answers, even if they are uncomfortable.

Very few situations and ruts are overcome as easily as as finding a new recipe or ordering pizza. Most require a lot of heavy lifting. Your nets may break. Things might get messy.

But the reward is so much greater than the sacrifice.

You and I weren't created to be stuck in the status quo. We were created to live life in motion, in abundance and to the full.

$$db$$

DAILY DARE

1. Identify the most pressing issue that is holding you back. What are the pros and cons of maintaining the status quo? What are the pros and cons of making a change? Write it down. Be honest with yourself and pray for the courage to act upon your findings.

2. If there is a relationship you have been avoiding or a conversation you need to have that you have been putting off, pick up your phone right now and make that call. Don't text! Our relationships are paramount and when neglected or abused, they can rob us of happiness, energy and hope. Take control of yours today. Do what is within your power to dig that relationship out of the rut and back on solid ground.

3. Move! Develop an action plan for climbing out of your rut. Hand over hand, foot over foot, write down the actions you can take to begin moving again—to begin living again. Every major movement begins with a footstep. Make yours today.

dare to

TURN THE PAGE

by **G**

DARE TO *TURN THE PAGE*

And I am convinced and sure of this very thing, that He Who began a good work in you will continue until the day of Jesus Christ, developing and perfecting and bringing it to full completion in you.

Philippians 1:6

Have you ever started reading a book only to drop it half-way through? Be it lack of time or commitment, boredom or distraction, you put the book down, ear-mark your spot and walk away with the best of intentions to return and finish the story.

Too often, though, we don't return. We never complete the story, leaving unfinished plots and half-developed characters inside those unread pages. Depending on our diligence to continue and the length of time we are distracted, that story can remain stuck for years or perhaps forever.

The journey of your life is like that book. It's a story that is developing and evolving. Each year, a new chapter is written, milestones are achieved and the adventure unfolds just a little more. Your personal growth and intentions determine the rate at which you continue writing your story. When we get distracted or weary, we have to resist the temptation of leaving it unfinished; of putting the pen down, of exiting our own story, of leaving pages forever unturned.

Yet, even when we are feeling uninspired or simply unable, everyday is an opportunity to turn the page, to write the next line. Each day presents new hope, strength, the potential of forging new relationships and discovering new scenery. It is our constant commitment to stay engaged in the story that opens up more possibilities.

Both of my children love to read—I mean love to read! They go through at least one book every two weeks. Yet, I have discovered that they also have become selective about what books they will read. If the author fails to develop a character, or the plot seems to meander for too long, they lose interest and start to read something else. I urge them to go back and finish the book they started, explaining they may just have to give the story a little more time to unfold, to appreciate that not every book has to start and finish the same way. But too often they abandon what they have deemed as boring to pick up something with a little more action.

Immaturity will have you compare your story with others. You don't have to look very far to find a plot you may prefer or a character with whom you would like to swap places.

Maturity knows that while not all stories unfold at the same pace, they do all have the same author. God is the one who holds the plot for your life. He doesn't want you to quit your story because it doesn't look like someone else's or isn't going the way you thought it would play out. Every one of our journeys will involve highs and lows; from valley to mountain top.

We all have a story to write and a page to turn. Today, don't envy someone else's storyline. Commit to writing yours well. Don't be overwhelmed by all the things you can't predict. Instead, invest yourself in whatever chapter you happen to be in and commit to the next page you can turn today. Dare to believe that your storyline is rich, relevant and ongoing. You never know what may await you further in this unfolding story; so read on!

DAILY DARE

1. If you were to give a title to the story of your life, what would it be and why?

2. Have you ever short-changed a possibility to write a new chapter in your own story because you were distracted by someone else's?

3. Make a commitment to share your journey with your Creator. Everyday, find time to read some of His story, pray about your own and trust that the author of every breath you take already knows the glories that your story will one day reveal.

dare to be

EXPECTANT

by ng

DARE TO BE *EXPECTANT*

The people were waiting expectantly and were all wondering in their hearts if John might possibly be the Messiah. John answered them all, "I baptize you with water. But one who is more powerful than I will come, the straps of whose sandals I am not worthy to untie."

Luke 3:15

When I hear the word, "expectant," my mind immediately goes to my babies. One of the greatest joys of my life was being an expectant mother. I remember sitting as still as possible to see if I could detect any movement. I remember singing to my belly and the baby inside. I remember dreaming about who this little human would someday become.

Expectancy is a wonderful thing. The definition is to have or show an excited feeling that something is about to happen, especially something pleasant and interesting.

If you've ever been around a six-year-old on Christmas Eve, you have likely witnessed expectancy personified. If you've ever been a six-year-old on Christmas Eve, you've likely personified expectancy.

Looking forward to something, feeling those butterflies in your stomach, counting the days until its arrival is wonderful and exciting. For many, however, it may seem more difficult to conjure any expectancy at all. A lifetime of hurts and disappointments can dull our sense of expectation. One too many let-downs can make us cynical. Sooner or later we stop looking for signs of good things to come. We convince ourselves that nothing's ever going to change and we must learn to live with it.

But God didn't create us to settle. We weren't made to be stagnant. We were and are meant to look to the horizon and see possibility; look to the Heavens and see a cosmos of wonders; look inside our own hearts and see the maker of Heaven and Earth who can do all things. Every day, we should keep our eyes wide-open, expecting to see the hand of God at work around us.

John the Baptist and his followers were an expectant lot. They knew the prophecies that foretold a Messiah. They believed what had been written about the coming King to be true and they waited with eyes wide open. When John the Baptist came along, the people noticed this man and his message and wondered if he was the One. John, of course, knew that his role was but to prepare the way for the true Messiah. He too expected the Savior to arrive soon. He kept watch and when Jesus came before him to be baptized, he immediately knew this was the One they'd been waiting for.

It's a beautiful absolution to such long-standing expectations. Perhaps one of the most profound details of the story is the length of time that passed between Isaiah's prophecy and Jesus' appearance.

700 years! (give or take)

For 700 years, the words that described the forthcoming Messiah remained in the forefront of the peoples' thoughts. And even after 700 years, so strong was their faith in the prophecy, they were still waiting with great expectation.

They hadn't grown cynical. They hadn't given up. They hadn't stopped looking for signs of the Promised One.

I know as well as anyone how easy it can be and how much safer it may seem to lower or eliminate expectations. If you never expect anything to happen, you'll never be disappointed, right?

Wrong!

We, who are made in the image of God, should be leading the charge when it comes to expecting great things. Because of the grace God has bestowed upon us, we have the hope of eternity within us. Our excitement and anticipation of Heaven should be palpable and evident to those around us. Likewise, our expectations of God's work in our lives here and now should be contagious.

Don't succumb to cynicism. Don't forfeit a dream or run from a calling out of fear that it may fall apart. The truth is, it might! But if it is something you have been called to by God, then expect Him to show up and work in mighty ways, even if those are hard to see at times.

Our God who moves mountains and paints the skies has great plans for you. Just like a mother dreams and hopes for her unborn child, you should have great expectations of yourself, your life and the God of possibility dwelling inside your heart.

DAILY DARE

1. Have you ever stopped yourself from expecting or hoping for a positive outcome just so you won't be disappointed if it were to fall through?

2. What are those things in your life you think about with great expectation and anticipation? Write them down. Whatever they may be, take your first step towards realizing each by getting them out of your head and into some kind of concrete, tangible form.

3. Pray every day for God to show up. Pray about any doubts you may harbor about who He is and how He loves you. Finally, pray for a childlike wonder and sense of excitement. Each day breaks into a new morning. Before you is a canvas of possibilities. Don't short-change yourself or the beautiful portrait your life was meant to become.

dare to be

STILL

by G

DARE TO BE *STILL*

"Be still, and know that I am God; I will be exalted
among the nations, I will be exalted in the earth."

Psalm 46:10

Have you ever seen a hyperactive child or had a thrill-seeking adrenaline junkie friend? Someone who is constantly moving, searching for the next activity, not prepared to slow down for the fear that it will somehow make life less amazing or appealing? Is that someone you? Can you recall the last time you actually stopped running to work, to kids, to church, to all of life's many events and just sat still? Or does that very idea make you feel incredibly uneasy? If so, you're not alone. In a world that constantly bombards our senses and demands our responses, action is the dominant MO. Stillness, on the other hand, is often under-appreciated and un-attempted!

Being still can almost sound like an old fashioned way of life and a sign you are becoming dull or possibly unexciting. Yet without stillness, we invite illness, sickness of soul and burn-out of body. We allow doing to replace being and our own well-being, relationships and families suffer when we cannot be still for long enough to sustain what is being entrusted to us.

Discerning the difference between busy and productive is often something we struggle with. Activity does not necessarily mean productivity. If we make opportunities, demands and prominence our goals, we will only strive and stress. We will replace real progress with our own manufactured semblance of success.

God calls us to a different kind of success or growth. The kind that can take place at home in the quiet or in the chaos of culture. True growth takes place when your sense of identity is not determined by what you do, but in whose you are. You'll be able to recognize your progress when you find that you are just as content in the still as you are in the crazy.

Wherever you are at this moment—still or not so much—consider the notion that the two aren't mutually exclusive. In fact, our busyness, our projects, our work of life cannot take place without the still. You may be able to offer short bursts every now and then, but it's not sustainable. Often a life that is all "go" lacks the "know." What we discover in the stillness carries us through the busyness. It is the knowledge of His greatness that quiets our neediness. When we are still, we can be refilled. When we are still, we can see wonder over works and spirit over self. If we are to increase our knowing, we must still our being. In all the many things you have to do, make room for this very important thing. Make time everyday to just be still, to say thank you to your Creator, to enjoy the things around you and to breathe in the possibilities and the future. It is in the stillness that you will find the ability to testify to all of God's greatness.

If we want to know more of Him today, we simply need to hear, see and consider less of ourselves. The truth is, God is constant, and His word foundational to you and your life in your busy and your stillness. But if we continually produce noise and excess for the sake of noise and excess, we can't hear anything beyond our own internal monologue, much less His voice. I dare you today to find a quiet place. Sit. Pray. Listen.

When your life is finally hushed enough to allow His love to echo through the chambers of your heart, the riches you discover will inevitably draw you closer to Him. Soon, the discipline of stillness will become a priority—a desire. The more you hear and know of Him the more you will want. As He calls you deeper still, the busyness around your life becomes somehow less important. What you do will began to matter less as you live more fully in the truth of who and whose you are. He is present with you right now. All you need to do is turn the volume down and allow Him to permeate your spirit, instilling you with the truth of His hunger for your heart.

Stillness breeds quiet. Quiet creates opportunity to listen, learn and know. Knowing Him is to love Him.

DAILY DARE

1. Does the thought of stillness and quiet make you uneasy? If so, why?

2. Is there a place in your life where you can simply sit, listen and be?

3. Stop talking about how you need to shut out the noise and overcome the chaos and literally begin shutting out the noise and removing the chaos. Pray for a desire to be still. And then pray for the understanding and capacity to listen and to know.

dare to

GIVE IT AWAY

by ng

DARE TO *GIVE IT AWAY*

And a ruler asked Him, "Good Teacher, what must I do to inherit
eternal life?" And Jesus said to him, "Why do you call me good?
No one is good except God alone. You know the commandments: 'Do not
commit adultery, Do not murder, Do not steal, Do not bear false witness,
Honor your father and mother.'" And he said, "All these I have kept
from my youth." When Jesus heard this, He said to him, "One thing
you still lack. Sell all that you have and distribute to the poor, and you
will have treasure in heaven; and come, follow me." But when he heard
these things, he became very sad, for he was extremely rich.

Luke 18:18-23 (ESV)

It never ceases to amaze me the simplicity, consistency and challenging manner in which Jesus addressed people while He was here on earth. He pulled no punches with this rich ruler. On the contrary, Jesus, the teacher known for using parables and metaphors, gave a straight-forward, tangible action-step that would open wide the gates of Heaven for this man. I have a sneaking suspicion that it had little to do with money; rather, Jesus was asking this man to sacrifice that which he held more dear than anything else—his possessions. Jesus knew that if this man could let go of that which he considered most precious, there would then be room in his heart for God.

He asks the same of you and me today. Our salvation isn't predicated on a list of do's and don't's. Rather, our relationship with God depends on us making room in our heart for Him. In other words, we must also sacrifice and surrender that which we hold most dear, understanding that there is nothing we can ever do to off-set the price of our salvation. Just look at the cross. Our salvation is priceless. There is no reparation equal to His sacrifice. Fortunately, that's not what He's seeking. All He wants is a vacancy inside our heart that His perfect love can fill.

But I know as well as anyone that that's a hard ask. Sometimes, I find myself scrambling to accomplish noble tasks so that, just as this ruler did, I can use them as leverage. Surely all these good things are adequate to cinch my salvation, right?

Of course not.

The ruler in this story did all the right stuff.

"But I've done all of that!" he said.

There's an immediate, almost knee-jerk response to defend his own actions (which Jesus never asked about).

I do the same thing. If there is a check list or some other system by which to measure my contributions, progress or activity, I'm going to clench it with an iron fist and let everyone know all that I've been doing to prove... what? I don't honestly know. Yet, it still seems important.

I've heard this story since I was a little girl, but only recently caught onto this. Before Jesus lists the commandments, there is no preface of "This is what you should do."

He wasn't giving us a task list or a road map. He simply made an observation. That young ruler knew all those rules. Jesus wasn't fact-checking for his sake. He was building up to the punchline—a poignant one that was really hard to swallow.

After the young ruler defended his track record, Jesus pointed out the one thing he lacked. One thing! Not a dozen or 44 or even two! There was ONE thing this young man had to do.

"Go sell what you own and give the money to the poor and you will have treasure in Heaven. Then, come and follow me."

The next verse sears me.

"When he heard this, he was shocked and went away grieving, for he had many possessions."

Let's zoom out a second here.

The thought of ridding himself of his stuff caused him to grieve. I don't know what losses you've experienced in your life. I've experienced many and I have been in the depths of despair and grief. Can you just for a moment wrap your head around the notion that becoming poor, ridding himself of wealth in exchange for eternity in Heaven was grief-inducing?

And there's another component here. Jesus says that once he has done that—sold his things, given to the poor—THEN he could follow him.

Jesus didn't and doesn't want divided attention. He wants all of us. He wants those pieces of our hearts that are deeply devoted and intertwined with something else—a relationship, possession, position, money. He is fully aware that while we continue to reserve a portion of our love, devotion and passion for something that is not Him, we can't truly be His.

You may recall one of the things Jesus says next. To paraphrase, "It's easier for a camel to go through the eye of a needle than for a rich man to enter heaven."

I'm no seamstress. I still have trouble threading a needle at times. And I use thread. Clearly the scenario Jesus paints here rests on the ridge of impossibility. A camel can't go through the eye of a needle—at least by no human power. Is it truly harder for a rich man to reach heaven?

I have no reason to doubt that it is. Which is why it is imperative that you and I take a long, hard look at our lives. What is it we treasure and build up? What do we cherish? What do we work for and spend our time earning? If it's wealth, it has to go. If it's position or notoriety, kick it to the curb. If it's another relationship, it needs to end or change.

Earlier in the book of Matthew, Jesus states that no one can serve two masters. "You cannot serve God and wealth."

That's pretty clear.

And very intimidating!

We live in a culture that revolves around money, accumulation, wealth, sustenance and privilege. How could we possibly turn our back entirely to the desire and need for money or possessions? Well, Jesus answers that too—we can't.

"For mortals, it is impossible, but for God all things are possible."

We can't get to a place of utter surrender and abandonment of worldly gain on our own. It's just not possible. But we can get to the foot of the cross. We can surrender our desires, ambition and vanity. We can pray. We can ask. We can listen until we hear an answer.

Giving up money isn't done lightly for me or anyone else.

The same is true for other treasures we cling to.

But I have a strong feeling that going to the cross to die for my sins and your sins wasn't done lightly. Nor was it easy. But it was done. And it was done for love. A love that we can't begin to comprehend here on earth. A love that literally went to hell and back so we wouldn't have to.

So when you look at your life and the ways you spend your time and energy, are they being spent in pursuit of Him and His will? If not, stop.

It's as simple and hard as that.

Don't abandon your responsibilities or put your family in jeopardy, but dare to be uncomfortable because of the amount you dare to sacrifice.

Dare to be without for a while.

Dare to be poor in this life for the riches and eternal wealth of the next.

DAILY DARE

1. What is your most prized possession or acquisition? Why?

2. When you wake up to go to work, what is your motivation? Ask yourself the hard question of why you do what you do and have the courage to be honest with yourself and with God.

3. Practice praying for a sacrificial spirit. Jesus said we can't do this without Him. Don't try. Today, right now, pray that your heart will bend in compassion to those who have less and that your hands will move to action to share from your table.

dare to be

EQUIPPED

by G

DARE TO BE *EQUIPPED*

"Write the vision; make it plain on tablets, so he may run who reads it."

Habakkuk 2:2

We all have dreams for our lives, mountaintops we are asking God to allow us to scale and views we desire to see. God wants you and me to dream. He gave Joseph dreams, woke Jacob with a dream, spoke to Cornelius in a dream, instructed Paul in a dream. God births dreams within us, but each dream God gives us comes with an assignment. We have to awaken the dream into its reality. Dreams require work, journey, commitment and sacrifice. Joseph's dream would have a huge price tag, taking him from pits to prisons to palaces. The summit he would eventually scale was one he would have to study from every angle—from humility to wisdom to stature. The same is true for us. God wants you and me to be dreamers who also become doers. He wants our faith to be accompanied by deeds so that we don't just talk about what we're going to do; we actually do it!

First things first. We'll never make those dreams come true, never climb that mountain in front of us if we're ill-equipped. We cannot scale to new heights without first embracing the disciplines that the mountain will demand. Often we fail to reach the summit because we spend more time visualizing the summit than developing the practical skills required to get there. How many climbs or projects have we embarked upon that we abandoned part-way in? Like climbers without the supplies to sustain them, we frequently venture out as inexperienced explorers when God is calling us to the mountaintops only seasoned mountaineers can scale. Each summit along the way is designed to teach and condition us. We must acclimatize to variations in altitude and train for the tougher terrain. Every one of these treks, big or small, serves to assess how well we are resourced in our attitude and commitment, patience and perseverance. Once we know where we are, we can begin acquiring new skills along the way.

Over the years, I have observed far too many casualties between the dream and the summit. I see ministries that become memorials to what someone once dared to dream, but never saw through. There are visions cast but not completed, impressive statements made without a strategy to bring them to life. We are called to continually become students of new and greater summits so that we can one day become guides for those who follow after us. What we see and what we learn should become visual and practical guides, full of wisdom to impart to new climbers long after our own summits have been conquered.

So today, commit to study the skills for the summit so that you can help more dreamers reach their summits too!

DAILY DARE

1. What is your summit today? What is your number one goal or desire? What's holding you back?

2. What skills or experience do you need to acquire in order to make it to the top?

3. Seek out others who have gone before you. Ask questions, learn from their experience and take their advice and best practices to heart. Then, set a date. Give your dream a deadline, make your punch-list and get to work!

dare to be

FORGIVING

by ng

But the man fell down before his master and begged him, "Please, be patient with me, and I will pay it all." Then his master was filled with pity for him, and he released him and forgave his debt. But when the man left the king, he went to a fellow servant who owed him a few thousand dollars. He grabbed him by the throat and demanded instant payment.

His fellow servant fell down before him and begged for a little more time. "Be patient with me, and I will pay it," he pleaded. But his creditor wouldn't wait. He had the man arrested and put in prison until the debt could be paid in full. When some of the other servants saw this, they were very upset. They went to the king and told him everything that had happened. Then the king called in the man he had forgiven and said, "You evil servant! I forgave you that tremendous debt because you pleaded with me. Shouldn't you have mercy on your fellow servant, just as I had mercy on you?" Then the angry king sent the man to prison to be tortured until he had paid his entire debt.

That's what my heavenly Father will do to you if you refuse to forgive your brothers and sisters from your heart.

Matthew 18:26-34 (NLT)

Has anyone ever told you that they're sorry for this, that or the other and you smile, say thanks or it's ok, all the while sensing that this person may not be sincere?

It's easy to say words... really, just about any words can be forced out of someone's mouth—even yours. Even mine! What's difficult is meaning them. Before you can mean them, you have to believe them. And when it comes to forgiving others, that's a difficult task indeed.

I once heard of a story in which a young woman lost her father in an accident. The woman responsible had been smoking marijuana, but because of the laws at the time in that state, she was found not-guilty. This young woman had an opportunity to speak to this woman at the trial. She looked into her face and said the words, "I forgive you." In fact, that was the headline of the local paper the next day.

Unfortunately, while it was probably a good start to utter the words, they hadn't become real yet for this girl. She hadn't yet come to a place where she was ready to forgive and, consequently, spent the next several years wrestling with her heart and conscience and this unplaced anger that had never been resolved. It had been shoved in a corner with a forgiven label slapped on top and left untended and unfinished.

That's a dangerous way to live. It's also practically the opposite of what Jesus demonstrated while He walked this earth and what His Father instructs us to do in His word. When Jesus was on the cross—nails in hands and feet, flesh ripped to shreds, thorns piercing His skull—He prayed that His Father would forgive the men who had just inflicted some of the most unspeakable pain and anguish anyone could ever experience.

Something tells me if He didn't mean it, He wouldn't waste what precious little energy He had left to utter words for the sake of optics.

He said those words because He meant them. In His greatest despair, He displayed a heart of forgiveness.

When I think back to various times in my life, I am humbled by the grace that has been bestowed upon me from my family, my friends, and of course, from my Savior. I have been showered in mercy and gifted with new chances over and over and over again.

Yet when I am wronged, it's easy to forget all the wrongs I've committed in the past. My eyes and heart can only focus on the immediate pain and anger.

There's an amazing example of this in scripture. A man owes a great debt to a king; one he can't pay. He begs for mercy and it is given. His debt is reconciled and his slate graciously wiped clean.

So what does he do? He immediately goes to someone who owes him money and does the exact same thing...

I'm just kidding.

On his way home, he runs into someone else who owes him money and demands payment. When the man can't pay, he has him thrown in jail. Ouch.

He does not show grace, mercy or compassion. He exudes self-importance, greed and apathy.

It's really easy to read that story and think horrible things about this man. Until I dwell on it for a minute and realize that I do the exact same thing time and time again. That realization certainly gives me pause as I consider the rest of that story.

As you can see in the above scripture, the original debt forgiver hears about this incident and immediately has the original debtor thrown in prison and tortured until he could satisfy his debt.

That's harsh. But possibly necessary. I think it's easy for many of us, particularly those of us who have grown up in church, to somehow think we've got a leg up on most of humanity. We pray, we attend church, we help with the PTA and volunteer at least a couple days a year. We're pretty good people. And when we're wronged, it should be righted.

We forget that we too are sinners. And in Christ's eyes, sin is sin is sin is sin. There's not a weighted system. You can't just commit a certain class of sins that's less bad than another. We are all sinners. Period. We all need grace. Period. We have all been given it. Period.

Thus, we have no grounds to hold a debt over the head of another.

Should people be held accountable for their actions? Of course.

How would anyone ever learn otherwise?

But should the wrongs of the past cloud everything about them? Of course not. They are still people. They are still God's children. They deserve love and forgiveness just as much as you or me.

For those of us who know Christ, we have an advantage. We have the power to pray, to seek the Holy Spirit's guidance, wisdom and discernment for our words, our thoughts and our intent.

Forgiving others isn't a choice we get to make. It's a mandate we either follow or we don't. And when we don't we're shortchanging ourselves on the glory that thrives on grace. We're missing out on the sweetest parts of life—those fueled by compassion and orchestrated by mercy. Forgiveness isn't lip service. You say it when you mean it and until you can do that, you pray until you get there.

We have been forgiven much. Far be it for us to deny grace to another.

db

DAILY DARE

1. Are there past hurts you're holding on to?

2. Can you name three people in your life who you need to forgive?

3. Write a letter. Pick up the phone or send an email to someone today who needs your forgiveness. They may not even realize there's an issue. That's ok. God wants you to be free. We can only do that when we exhibit and live out of the overflow of grace that has already washed us clean.

dare to

NOT DO NOTHING

by G

DARE TO *NOT DO NOTHING*

I once walked by the field and the vineyard of a lazy fool. Thorns and weeds were everywhere, and the stone wall had fallen down. When I saw this, it taught me a lesson: Sleep a little. Doze a little. Fold your hands and twiddle your thumbs. Suddenly poverty hits you and everything is gone!

Proverbs 24:30-34

A picture may paint a thousand words, but these words sure do paint a compelling image. I'm picturing a guy in overalls with his hat over his eyes getting a nap in...in the middle of the day. (Clearly I've placed a contemporary filter on my imagery!)

Whatever the time period, the idea of someone dozing off isn't in itself that egregious of a misstep. If you look at the context, however, the weeds and crumbling walls indicate that this wasn't a one-time thing. Sure, his nap wasn't necessarily hurting anything; but it sure wasn't helping. His relatively benign negligence opened the gate for harmful things to enter in, overtaking what once was fertile soil.

I suppose the old adage is true—if you're not helping, you're hurting.

Doing nothing is not neutral. Where we fold our arms, weeds grow. Where we fall asleep, walls come down. If we aren't invested in our own lives, they go nowhere. When we spend our days twiddling our thumbs, surfing Facebook, comparing our lives to everyone else's, we're neglecting what we've been entrusted with. While our thoughts are occupied with everyone else's achievements, possessions and position, our own falls into disrepair. We're not necessarily sabotaging ourselves on purpose, but before we know it, our habit of apathy regarding our own affairs leads to weeds—not fruit. As we soon find out, the work of neglect is often much more expensive than the work of diligence.

Much like the "fool" mentioned in the Proverb, neglect makes us vulnerable, but does so discreetly. We often think an outside attack will destroy what we have labored to build; yet we fail to be aware of the internal damage that can be caused when we allow what we have been entrusted with to be ignored or unprotected. Your family, marriage or business are zones that God has entrusted to you to grow and maintain, tend to and establish. Yet if we do not own our zone, something else will. Weeds will grow, disrepair and damage will occur.

I learned first-hand just how not-neutral our apathy can be; how it can place the ground we have previously taken in jeopardy. Once, when my son was sick and running a fever, I sent him to bed to sleep it off (no, I'm not the best nurse). Later I went to check in on him and the fever was worse. Now a little more concerned, I prayed over him as he slept. The best way to describe my prayer was short and sweet. As I left his room, I felt the Holy Spirit speak to me, saying, "Is that it? Is that the kind of prayer you are praying? Go back and take authority over this situation." Those words awakened what had become routine, dormant and subsequently apathetic in me. Realizing that nothing changes if it is not challenged, I went back in that bedroom and prayed with passion and authority that no sickness was welcome in my zone. To my surprise the fever broke and my son even said from his deep sleep, "Amen." It seems his body was asleep but his spirit was wide-awake and waiting for me to wake-up too.

We have to own the zone of our relational world if we want to keep it from thistle and thorns. Complacency and apathy have no place in a life you hope to be fruitful and shared with others. What God has given to you— your home, your family, your skills—is a precious, direct outpouring of His grace and favor. It should be honored and cared for with passion, respect and expectation. Anything less shortchanges your gifts, your relationships and the grace God has designated just for you.

DAILY DARE

1. Can you identify areas of your life that are vulnerable and open to infestation?

2. What have you grown complacent about? Are there aspects of your faith, work, relationships that have become so routine they are practically mindless?

3. Think about what it means to take ownership of your life. Pray for apathy to dissipate from your heart and mind. Practice passion. Commit to courageously owning all that God has given you.

dare to be

FORGIVEN

by ng

DARE TO BE *FORGIVEN*

Therefore, if anyone is in Christ, the new creation has come:
The old has gone, the new is here!

2 Corinthians 5:17

If someone were to record your internal monologue, would you want your children or other loved ones to hear it? Do you speak to yourself and think of yourself in ways that edify? Would you ever say to someone else what you say to yourself?

There are times when my self-talk is anything but encouraging or positive. I'm of the type that tends to universalize just about every small issue. Mommy-guilt gets the best of me from time to time. Before long and without even realizing it, I have defined myself as one who is less than worthy. I can become so consumed with this narrative that I forget that the greatest act of love—Jesus' sacrifice on the cross—was done for me, too. It wasn't just my sin that put Him on a cross. It was His love and grace that led Him to sacrifice everything for me.

It was His decision as my Maker and Creator to offer grace. Even in the midst of my darkest sin, He decided that I would no longer be defined by my wrongs. Rather, I could be defined by His action—forgiveness.

Every morning when I rise and at night when I lay down, I do so as one who has been forgiven.

That's head knowledge that I can espouse all day long. I know just about every scripture there is that proclaims mercy. I know that His blood has washed me clean.

But there's often a disconnect between knowing and believing.

One of my favorite stories in the Bible is a story of a woman who bridges that gap before our very eyes. In the span of a few verses, she not only learns about grace; she accepts it, believes it and can't wait to share it.

It's a story you probably know well. The Samaritan woman at the well has become synonymous with grace and compassion. I find her particularly relatable because we first meet her when she's existing in a downward spiral of unworthiness and shame. When Jesus first lays eyes on her, she is drawing water from a well in the middle of the day. That's significant! It was hot in the middle of the day. Drawing water was hard work and not something most people chose to do when the sun was at its peak, which is exactly the reason she was there at that time. She was doing what I sometimes want to do—she was hiding.

She knew that everyone else knew about her past and her mistakes and her shame. She'd likely lived a lot of life as the subject of ridicule and defamation. She'd heard the whispers of other women in the community as she walked by. She knew all too well what the men must have thought as she passed through town.

I can only imagine her internal monologue.

Jesus didn't have to. He knew exactly who she was, what she had done and the pain her choices had brought upon her life. Despite it all, though, He chose to see her as a child of God. He chose to take the time to listen, to help her process and to show her kindness. He chose to forgive her, to give her living water...to show her another way to live.

There are so many parts of this story that are simply mind-blowing. The first is socio-political. She was a Samaritan woman. Jews did not have dealings or interaction of any kind with Samaritans.

Except Jesus.

She was known to have had many husbands. She had a reputation. And when people weren't talking about her, they were shunning her.

Except Jesus.

She had made mistakes. She had done things that no one could forgive.

Except Jesus.

Notice a pattern?

The same is true for you and me.

I make mistakes. You make mistakes. Some can feel debilitating.

In those moments, I cling to the truth that woman discovered that day at the well—except Jesus.

When I stare into the mirror at a face I feel has fallen too far, those words are a life line.

Except Jesus.

Except Jesus.

Except Jesus.

Those two words remind me that I am not my past. I am not my sin. I am forgiven. If ever my thoughts start to drift into that danger zone of self-loathing or negativity, I have to remind myself that those things short-change what Jesus did on the cross.

He died to forgive me.

Who am I to decide that it wasn't enough?

Who am I to claim that my sin is too great...that my worth is too small?

The woman at the well gives me hope. Her response to Jesus inspires me. Her first action was to run into the village to proclaim to all the people she had tried to avoid that this man knew everything about her and had shown her love.

God knows everything about me. He knows everything about you. And His knowledge doesn't evoke judgment. His knowledge evokes mercy. It is because He knows our everything that He sent His son to the cross. His sacrifice washed away the labels, the whispers and the cold shoulders. His sacrifice means that you and I are whole. We are His. We are forgiven.

DAILY DARE

1. Have you done things in your past you haven't been able to move beyond? Write them down. Be honest and thorough.

2. What do those events evoke within you? Do they make you feel shame? Do they cause you to doubt your self-worth? Write down how you perceive yourself in light of these mistakes. Be specific.

3. Now start a new list. Write down all of the ways God sees you. What does He call you? Who does He say that you are? Compare your lists, hold on to truth and pray everyday for the capacity to live in the fullness of forgiveness.

dare to

FILL YOUR HEART FIRST

by G

DARE TO *FILL YOUR HEART FIRST*

Delight yourself in the Lord, and He will give you the desires of your heart.

Psalm 37:4

Your heart should be fuller than your hands at all times. When the reverse is true, we are bound to become weary, burdened and battered. Our grip begins to weaken. Everything in our hands—relationships, responsibilities, resources—is now in a precarious situation. When our heart is running on empty but our hands remain full, we are heading for trouble. Something or someone will get dropped. Somewhere along the way, we will feel more resentment than enjoyment and begin to complain about the things we previously volunteered to carry.

Fueling your heart with good things is not an annual event, nor should it be an emergency pit-stop. Rather, it is a daily discipline. We must choose to delight ourselves in the Lord before we become overwhelmed with our tasks. We need to make the space to meditate on His words, sing songs of thanksgiving and think on all He has done for us. Our heart needs to be filled with joy, compassion and worship so that our hands can become a way to externally reflect the internal heart-work already taking place. If you are doing more but spending less time to refuel, eventually you will find yourself out of sync, spiritually. When our hands are full but our heart is empty, we no longer enjoy; we simply endure.

A while ago I was driving our car and I noticed the fuel was getting a little low, but because I decided I didn't have time to refuel due to the appointment I was already running late for, I ignored the sign and kept driving. I took that sign as a suggestion, although in reality it was trying to save me. It was letting me know to stop before I got in trouble; to get fuel so I could keep going. What I saw as an interruption was actually an instruction to help me, not hinder me. Sure enough, the more I ignored that flashing light, the more damage I did to the engine of that car and with only fumes left in the tank, the next person who tried to use the car discovered that my irresponsibility had now become their huge inconvenience, as they had to address what I had ignored.

It is a necessary part of life to refuel. Everything in your hands will benefit from you making a heart-stop. Everything that has been dragging will gain new momentum. We all have so many things placed in our hands to do, but only you and I can take on the work of filling our hearts. Don't let others' enthusiasm to fill your hands be greater than your own dedication to fill your heart. Let's be heart-full before we are hands-full.

DAILY DARE

1. What's the reading on your spiritual gas gauge? Are you in need of a pit-stop?

2. Do you have a habit of running and running until you're literally coasting on fumes? How has this effected your productivity or relationships?

3. Commit to a daily re-fill. Read a few verses. Say a quick prayer. Start somewhere, doing something today. Commit to keeping your heart full, so your hands can do the work for which they have been commissioned.

dare to be

WRONG (OUT LOUD)

by ng

DARE TO BE *WRONG (OUT LOUD)*

Nicodemus said to him, "How can a man be born when he is old?
Can he enter a second time into his mother's womb and be born?"

John 3:4

I've heard it said that if you're going to make a mistake, make it loud enough or big enough for someone else to notice. Why? You can't fix what you don't know is broken.

I don't relish being wrong, but I have found freedom in drawing attention to my flaws. I find it to be humbling, but also humanizing.

If I never put myself out there...never took a guess or a chance or a risk... I'd never get anywhere. I might save face (or feel like it) at the time, but I wouldn't learn or grow.

Speaking of learning, I'm gonna go out on a limb and guess one of the first Bible verses you ever learned was John 3:16. Say it with me!

"For God so loved the world He gave His only begotten Son, that whosoever believes in Him shall not perish but have everlasting life."

How'd you do? Kudos to you!

Here's another one—do you know or remember the verses that immediately precede that one? I knew the story but didn't realize the context until recently. Jesus is sharing the birthing process with a Jewish leader, Nicodemus; specifically, the "born-again" birthing process.

The conversation takes place one evening when Nicodemus seeks out Jesus. He had heard murmurs about being born-again and, while he was aware of and believed in the miracles Jesus had performed, he didn't really get the whole new-birth thing. Which is completely legitimate!

You and I have likely grown up in the rhetoric of the church. Being "born-again" is as common a phrase as "pass the plate." It's part of the whole church package. Yet Nicodemus didn't attend an evangelical seminary or learn from a flannel-gram in VBS. This was a new concept. And it was weird. And Nicodemus had the intelligence and wherewithal to say out-loud to this great man of God that he didn't know the answer. He didn't understand.

That's impressive! Even more so when you read Jesus' response in verse ten.

Jesus answered him, "Are you the teacher of Israel and yet you do not understand these things?"

Awkward...

In other words, given his position and reputation, you'd think he would have a grasp on this whole concept. Nonetheless, he didn't. And when he asked, he learned! Jesus explained what it means to be born of the spirit. And wouldn't you know Nicodemus' tutoring session would become one of the most well-known, pivotal lessons millions and millions of people have committed to heart for generations. You guessed it: "For God so loved the world..."

It's never easy to admit when you're wrong or you don't know the answer. But it's a lot worse to remain willingly ignorant. You never know what you never know. And you never know when your questions and curiosity and your mistakes can turn into a life-lesson for yourself and/or for someone else.

So if you're going to sing, sing loud. If you're going to speak, make your voice be heard. And if you're going to choose to remain open to instruction, receptive of constructive criticism and willing to change course, you just might wind up with some of the greatest knowledge you never knew you didn't have.

DAILY DARE

1. Can you think of a time when you were wrong or didn't know the answer to something? How did you feel in that moment?

2. Ask yourself how you feel about asking for help, direction or feedback. Are you open? Are you indignant? Be honest with yourself about your capacity to receive instruction.

3. Pray for an open and curious heart. Pray that the pursuit of knowledge will be one of encouragement and excitement; not one of embarrassment. Pray that you will have the discernment to know when you don't know and the resolve to seek wise council.

dare to

KEEP HIS RHYTHM

by G

DARE TO *KEEP HIS RHYTHM*

Are you tired? Worn out? Burned out on religion? Come to me.
Get away with me and you'll recover your life. I'll show you how to take
a real rest. Walk with me and work with me—watch how I do it. Learn
the unforced rhythms of grace. I won't lay anything heavy or ill-fitting
on you. Keep company with me and you'll learn to live freely and lightly.

Matthew 11:28-30 (MSG)

Have you ever been on a dance floor and, even though you may not be the world's greatest dancer, at that moment, you are Fred Astaire all the way (or one of the Hough siblings), compared to the person next to you? Bless their heart; it's as if they are immune to the beat and allergic to the rhythm.

As the wife of a former professional drummer and accomplished percussionist, I know what it is to appreciate the rhythm in a song. My husband can't cope if I even clap out of time. He is like the rhythm police! And deservedly so! After years of training with symphonies around the world, he understands if you lose the rhythm, you lose the power and cohesion of the whole piece.

If this is God's great dance floor that we are on, then God is our great dance instructor. God has a rhythm to bring cohesion to the set-piece of your life. He knows the tempo for the season you are currently in. He is the conductor of the orchestra and the master of the score. All we have to do is let Him lead. He sent His Spirit to teach us not just how to get through life but how to do it with the "unforced rhythms of grace."

All across the world people ask me the same question: "How do you do all you do and stay sane?" While the sane part is disputable, the first part I have learned to answer from this verse in Matthew. I have stopped working for God and learned how to work with Him. That changes everything. So instead of giving people my five top tips on juggling life and all its demands, I simply quote this verse and say, "I have learned how to dance in time to God's music."

In encouraging others to do the same, I would never presume to tell anyone how to run their home or schedule their lives. My rhythm probably isn't your rhythm and vice-versa. We can learn from each other but we can't take the job of the Holy Spirit, who longs to teach you the tempo for your life.

Today, whatever you are heading out to do, make sure it's "with Him." Walk "with Him," not ahead or away from Him. Talk "with Him," not just about or around Him. Be "with Him," not just doing for Him. The "with Him" will ease the tension and increase the rhythm of grace. If we want to dance better we have to be willing to move closer to the instructor and follow His lead. Grace is the timeless and unconditional rhythm of life. It holds you in the fast-paced jive moments and it settles you into the slower waltz seasons. It starves the striving and feeds the trusting. It patiently and consistently gives you the right beat at the right tempo for every moment. He's not looking for you to win the mirror ball on "Dancing With the Stars." He simply wants to invite you onto the dance floor, into His arms, swaying to the perfect, divine rhythm of His love.

DAILY DARE

1. Where do you lack rhythm in your marriage, career, parenting or leadership role?

2. Does the idea of handing over the reigns and letting someone else—even God Himself—lead scare you? Excite you? Challenge you? Think about what it means to be a partner with God. If something is holding you back, try to discover the source of the issue and how to dispel it.

3. Pray to be in sync with your Savior and Creator. Listen for His rhythm, follow His lead and let the world see how our faithful Father holds us so perfectly in His arms, swaying to the dance He's choreographed for you and you alone.

dare to be

SILENT

by ng

DARE TO BE *SILENT*

Whoever belittles his neighbor lacks sense,
but a man of understanding remains silent.

Proverbs 11:12

You can learn a lot about someone in the first three seconds you are in their car. In those moments, you get a glimpse, or an earful at least, of what that person does while they're on their own. Some have the radio blaring. Others have NPR on. Still, others have nothing on.

While any and all of the above are great—to each their own—have you ever tried to say something to the driver in scenario one? How'd that conversation go? I'd imagine not too far until the music was turned down.

Not because the music is bad.

Not because your hearing is bad.

Not because anything is bad at all.

It's common sense. You can't hear someone else when their voice is being drowned out.

Over time, I have come to not only value, but to crave quiet. It hardly needs to be said, but we live in a world and culture that is loud. Media is everywhere. Our personal lives are ruled by devices that ring, whistle, tweet or play some annoying ring-tone we can't figure out how to change. Our increased social connectedness has effected nearly every aspect of nearly everything from politics to pop culture to our own well-being.

It's not all bad, mind you. I'm never at a loss for driving directions. I can catch up on news anytime I want and, if necessary, I can take my office with me.

Bottom line—I benefit a lot from the cacophony that is the background of our lives. At the same time, I can not only get sucked into the maelstrom of noise and chaos, I can become part of it. It's far too easy to convince myself that if I am to survive in this hurricane of sound, I must be louder. My voice has to somehow rise to the top in order for me to feel relevant. Day after day, I take it up a notch. And then another. And then another. Until I can not only hear my voice—I can hear nothing else.

That's dangerous.

When the only feedback I'm sensing and processing is my own, I'm setting myself on a course of stagnation, complacency and futility. How can I learn new things if I am my own life coach?

I can't. No one can.

Enter the sanctuary that is the silence of my vehicle. When I close those doors and roll up the windows, I suddenly have nothing with which to compete. I can just be. Those moments, void of sound, not only give my ears a break; they give my voice a break, inviting me to savor the silence.

However, if all I'm doing in the quiet is being, well, quiet, I'm missing an opportunity. Many times throughout scripture, we read stories of men and women who retreat to a solitary and silent space. In not one of those stories is the objective simply to escape the noise. The purpose is to listen.

In 1 Kings, we read about the dramatic saga of the prophet Elijah. He had some stuff going on! His life was loud...much of the noise provided courtesy of Queen Jezebel, who thought life would be better with one less prophet in the world. During one of her attempts to ascertain her nemesis, Elijah, he retreats. Actually, 1 Kings 19:3 says he "ran for his life." Eventually he found his way to a cave. There, he experienced an earthquake, a fire and a windstorm.

After the chaos, a stillness descended. Within it, a still, small voice could be heard. It was—you guessed it—the voice of God, telling Elijah what to do next.

Have you felt like Elijah lately? Do you feel like you're running for your life, seeking refuge in caves or foxholes? Is the noise of your life bringing you to a stand-still, unable to discern what's right, what's wrong or what's next?

I urge you to seek a place of solitude and honor it. Create a place to go in your house, your neighborhood or even in your car where the noise can be shut out. Don't bring your phone, your iPad, your laptop or even your kids. You deserve, but more importantly, you need to create quiet, to listen.

You can't control the circumstances around you. You can't control the noise others are making. But you can control your own tongue. You can control whether or not you seek out or create an environment that makes listening possible.

The next time you find yourself speaking or yelling so loudly you hear nothing else, take a step back. Ask yourself if you're being productive or just adding to the noise. Chaos breeds chaos. Break the cycle. Listen more than you speak and prime your ears for a still, small voice longing to lead you.

$$db$$

DAILY DARE

1. Think about your daily routine. Can you identify any periods of time that allow for quiet or solitude? If not, adjust your schedule. Set an appointment with yourself daily to simply be away from the noise.

2. Are there any locations in your home or community where you can shut a door, turn off the phone and simply be quiet? Create one. Find one. Go there everyday. Let your family know that this is your time and space to take care of yourself and to be your best for them.

3. How long can you go without saying a word? Don't laugh. I dare you to carve out five minutes every day to say absolutely nothing and just listen. Add ten minutes each week. Pay attention to the changes in your life as you honor your need for respite and reflection.

dare to be

THOUGHTFUL

by G

DARE TO BE *THOUGHTFUL*

Our Lord, everything you do is kind and thoughtful,
and you are near to everyone whose prayers are sincere.

Psalm 145:17-18

Have you ever received a gift that is so beautifully presented, you get just as much enjoyment from looking at it as you do once you get to open it? The time and attention that has gone into the gift-wrapping process lets you know this gift wasn't just given; it was beautifully and thoughtfully prepared. The choice of paper and bows adds another layer of beauty and love. Those are the gifts that get the front and center spot under the tree. It's the kind you open carefully so you can save the paper for the next gift you give.

Thoughtfulness is like that wrapping paper. It turns something ordinary into something very special; something usual into something unusual.

Whether we are presenting a message, a lesson, a gift or a meal, it's the thoughtfulness that takes into account the things beyond the task itself. It goes further than the thing that needs doing; it determines how it will be done. You can tell the difference between food served by a stranger, eager to move you along for the sake of more tips, and a time sitting down to eat with the ones you love. Yes, the food matters; but the context determines and can change the purpose and function of a meal. One that is served with care, love and in fellowship is not only nourishing your body; it's refreshing your soul.

Thoughtfulness, attention to detail and a heart bent towards service is like God's gift-wrap. When we use it, everything we do looks, sounds and tastes better. For example, you can correct your children on the fly or you can give thought into how that correction is delivered, received and followed through. Likewise, you can share your story to anyone at anytime; or you can take time and soak that same story in thought and prayer.

By taking the time to step back, think and enhance whatever it is you're about to do, you will inevitably find new ideas, thoughts and ways to make that expression even more powerful and moving. In writing, I would never publish a first draft of anything. Instead, I take that first draft, analyze it, correct it, refine it, seek input and only then begin to round out the story in a style worthy of the message.

At the end of the day, most of us want to be thoughtful, careful and caring people and communicators. The problem, however, is that thoughtfulness takes more time. We often just want to give as we go. We throw out one lesson while we are simultaneously moving onto the next. In doing so, we shrink the potential impact we're trying so hard to achieve. It's a quantity over quality catch-22, in which the former frequently wins out, denigrating the latter. While much of today's culture subscribes to the more is better concept, it is practically the antithesis of Jesus' approach to people, ideas and lessons.

Jesus took time to wrap His miracles in grace, tie them up in love and present them in ways that were as creative as they were constructive. Once He healed a blind man with a word; another with clay placed over his eyes. Jesus turned water into wine at the very beginning of His ministry; a few years later, He spent time with a woman who was thirsty and asked her to drink from a deeper well. Jesus' teaching was unlike the religious scholars who quoted laws and cast judgements. Jesus' teaching was thoughtfully wrapped in stories that people could understand and connect with—stories that made sense in their everyday world. From parables about sowing seed to sorting sheep, He took the time to think about how He would share—not just what He would say.

His example should prompt us to do likewise. Our thoughtfulness should create a sense of comfort and belonging to those who don't know Jesus at all. Our care should demonstrate the sincerity of the words we speak. Our time should be spent focusing upwards and outwards—not merely inwards.

Today, I dare you to be mindful of your interaction with others and the actions you make. Are you merely giving the world words that ultimately come across as hollow? Bottom line—presentation matters. Attention to detail makes a difference. Thoughtfulness may be the crux upon which the success of our words resides. Our world needs to see that we, as the church, care and that we take the time not just to preach our points, but to wrap our actions and words in love. Thoughtfulness makes each gift we give more attractive for others to receive. Where can you add a layer of thoughtfulness today?

d_b

DAILY DARE

1. Can you think of a gift you've received that was wrapped or presented so beautifully, one look and you immediately knew it had taken some time for the gift-giver to create the presentation. What struck you the most about the gift or the gift-giver?

2. If the last conversation you had with a friend or loved one was represented as a present, how would you rate the wrapping job? Would it be pristine, without creases or strange bumps and lumps with an intricate bow on top? Or would it look something like a wrinkled mess—the kind where you're not quite sure if it's a lump of trash or some misshapen lump with a gift inside? Either way, how would you describe the reaction of the receiver?

3. If your schedule is so full that you feel you don't have time to put lots of thought or meticulous detail into something or someone, consider areas or tasks that can be eliminated. Remember—quality over quantity!

dare to be

HUMBLED

by ng

DARE TO BE *HUMBLED*

My soul glorifies the Lord and my spirit rejoices in God my Savior,
for He has been mindful of the humble state of His servant.

Luke 1:47-48

Humble - adjective - having or showing a modest or low estimate of one's own importance.

Humbled - verb - lower (someone) in dignity or importance.

As a writer of songs and stories, I absolutely love and truly cherish the power of language; in particular, the nuances of the words we speak, write or sing. The meaning of a word can be completely changed with the addition or subtraction of a single letter.

Take the word humble. In its primary iteration, it's an adjective, defined as having or showing a modest or low estimate of one's own importance.

Doesn't that sound awesome? Don't you love humble people and want others to think of you in that light? Being humble is a virtue.

On the other hand, add a "d" to the end of the word and you're dealing with something completely different. To be humbled is a verb. It's the action of lowering someone in dignity or importance. To be humbled is uncomfortable. But if I'm truly striving for a state of humility, I can't also avoid criticism and learning opportunities simply so I don't have to feel anything less than great about who I am. The two negate each other.

In my estimation, there is practically no more beautiful example of humility than Mary, the teenager chosen to birth the Son of God.

Personally, I can hardly contain myself when my kids do amazing things. If they know all their vocabulary words for school, I turn into a one-woman pep rally! If they hold a door for someone behind them, I'm convinced that their emotional IQ is off the charts.

I can only assume that you feel the same way about your children. Or if you don't have kids, there is probably someone in your life that you are proud of; someone whose accomplishments leave your mouth hanging open.

Just imagine being told that that special person or your own child was going to be the Son of God, the long-awaited Messiah. I'm pretty sure there wouldn't be a wall in a five-mile radius I wouldn't be bouncing off of. And what personal pride I would feel to be chosen! All of which is probably why Mary was a much stronger choice than someone like me. Her response was not only gracious and modest; it was incredibly risky!

Upon hearing the news of her forthcoming pregnancy, Mary accepted the task willingly, modestly and with an inspiring humility. In doing so, she literally put her life on the line. She would be an unwed, pregnant teenager. It wasn't unusual for women to be exiled or even killed for a pregnancy outside of marriage. She would have to explain to her fiancé that the conception process was not carnal, but divine. She was brave. With a bowed head and a modest heart, Mary accepts and responds with gratitude, all the while knowing full well that she was about to be humbled—lowered in dignity—among her family and friends. Her status would be forever changed. She willingly, even gratefully, decided to forsake her own reputation for her child, her Savior, her God.

Mary's actions and reactions are a beautiful foreshadowing of decisions her son, Jesus, would make throughout His earthly life. He washed His disciples' feet. He served them. He spoke to people of low social status. He went to the cross. This humble Savior, Son of God, Creator of the universe prioritized those whom society had deemed unimportant or unworthy. In doing so, He humbled Himself. He willingly sacrificed His dignity, His status, His life on the cross.

Why? Because there's no price He wouldn't pay to show His love to you.

I'll never claim to be a theologian, but when I consider the behavior of Mary and Jesus, mother and son, I can't help but think the willingness to be humbled isn't merely an admirable character trait; it's a mandate. I think I am called to be willing to forfeit my social status and/or my personal dignity should God say the word. I know that's easier said than done. Should that time ever come, I'll know what I should do and I can only pray I have the personal fortitude to follow through.

What about you? What are you willing to sacrifice for your King? How low are you willing to bow in the name of obedience?

It's a wonderful thing to be a humble person. It is exceedingly more difficult to be a humbled person. But God hasn't called us to do what is easy. Being a pregnant, unwed teen wasn't easy. The cross wasn't easy. But they were necessary.

Today, thousands of years later, the hard stuff is still necessary. The sacrifice of personal pride and dignity is imperative if we truly desire to know His will, seek it and act upon it.

DAILY DARE

1. Can you think of someone in your life who is truly a humble person? What is it about them that sets them apart?

2. Has there been a time when you have been called to sacrifice personal dignity for the sake of something greater than yourself?

3. How would your life be different if you were no longer concerned about social status and standing? Pray for a heart willing to be more than modest; pray for the willingness to follow the example of Christ—to be humbled, even unto the cross.

dare to

DIVE DEEP

by G

DARE TO *DIVE DEEP*

God's love is meteoric, His loyalty astronomic, His purpose titanic,
His verdicts oceanic. Yet in His largeness nothing gets lost;
Not a man, not a mouse, slips through the cracks.

Psalm 36:5-9 (MSG)

Have you ever found yourself at the edge of a cliff, terrified at what may be below but compelled to seriously consider taking the plunge? I think we're all there from time to time. Every day we walk through moments in between the unknown and the familiar. We know we eventually need to leave what has become safe, but there are some major hesitations and questions when it comes to actually taking that first step. While fear is a common and logical culprit, more often than not, it's things like our time, doubts, questions or even our own sense of control or lack thereof that anchor us to the ground. That part of us that wants and seemingly needs to be in charge interferes with the other part of us compelling us to jump in.

God has another plan. He consistently brings us to a precipice of new discovery and asks only that we allow trust instead of fear or interference to overwhelm our hearts and guide our decisions. When He places us in front of waterfalls of possibilities and oceans of revelation, we have a choice to make. We either take a selfie at the edge or jump in, learn how to swim and then go deeper.

Where are you standing right now? What are you at the edge of? In what area of your life are you a little scared of the next step? Do you need to stop living off drops of patience and start swimming in it? Do you need to replace your bucket of grace with oceans? Do you need to throw yourself into something you have been paddling on the edge of? Swim in forgiveness, get drenched in His presence. Jump past familiar; get under the waterfall of God's beautiful adventure.

All of us have a choice—play it safe or live beyond the easy and comfortable, committing to the task of expanding our own capacity and ability to trust—even if we fail. The reality is that failure is an important part of our journey. It teaches us many lessons in a way nothing else can. If we live so cautiously that we never even have a chance of failing, we develop a false sense of security and replace trust in God with pride and security in our own limited abilities.

Think about it. A child will never learn to walk unless we allow them to fall over and over again as they try to move from crawling to standing and standing to walking. The same is true for a bird destined to soar in open skies; it will never know what's within it until it is made to leave what is familiar for what literally looks like falling into nothing. It will never find its wings unless it's tossed out of the nest. Yes, safe is tidy and can even look like success. But no matter how far or fast you run, is it truly success when you were created to fly?

Today, be brave with your life and allow Him to nudge you forward where control and fear have held you back. Let's not settle for good when we can experience great. Let's not allow what once was our edge of new to now become our wall of forever. Where do you need to leave safe and embrace a little scary? Remove the weights that are keeping you from making the leaps of faith for which you are destined and see just how far you can fly.

DAILY DARE

1. Where are you playing it safe in your life? Are there risks you are avoiding for fear of failure?

2. If there was an absolute guarantee that you could not fail, what would you dream of doing?

3. Pray for and pursue a life that is as bold, daring and deep as is our God.

dare to be

DELAYED

by ng

DARE TO BE *DELAYED*

*Jesus said, "Let the little children come to me, and do not hinder them,
for the kingdom of heaven belongs to such as these."*

Matthew 19:1

Do you remember the last time you were stuck in traffic on your way to a really important meeting? Fun, wasn't it?

I'm kidding. Who likes to be stuck on the road? It throws off our schedule. It's frustrating.

Nearly every adult I know adheres to an agenda. At the same time, nearly every child I know, doesn't.

If we're out and about and run into a friend from school or church, my daughters make a bee-line towards their friends, immediately and exponentially more excited and interested in socializing than grocery shopping.

If we happen to drive by a Chick Fil A, it seems completely logical to them that we should immediately pull over, get some waffle fries and hit up the Play Place. In their mind, what could possibly be more important or urgent than indulging in such pleasantries? While I never relish the verbal tug of war that ensues when such a request is made, I hope I can always remember their innocence and unassuming quest for delight whenever and wherever.

It's a beautiful thing to watch a child who is attuned to their internal instinct for food, company and fun. Sadly, it's a virtue most of us grow out of far too soon. I don't mean that everyone should drop all their "have-to's" in order to get to the "want to's." I simply feel that as we get older, become more socially aware and culturally conscious, our lives are increasingly dictated by the clock and less by our divinely-endowed human nature.

Throughout scripture, there are lots of stories that have an element of time management to them. Some are sweet. Some are convicting. All are good food for deep thought.

In Matthew 19, Jesus and His disciples had just arrived in Judea after a long journey from Galilee. Nearly as soon as they set their feet on Judea's soil, crowds began flocking to Jesus. Among them were children.

In my head, I've always pictured that moment looking something like the line of kids waiting to sit on Santa's lap. The disciples did not agree with my rose-colored interpretation of the event. Rather, they rebuked the children, seeing them as a nuisance and an unnecessary delay in their "Jesus Across Judea" tour.

Jesus disagreed.

He not only told his entourage to step aside so the kids could come forth; He used them as an example!

What the disciples thought was an unnecessary delay, Jesus used to teach a necessary lesson.

Another instance in scripture revolves around a visit to close friends, Martha and Mary. Jesus was at their home to fellowship and Mary popped a squat right next to Him to listen to His wisdom and stories. Martha, on the other hand was busy, busy, busy in the kitchen, making sure the house was presentable and, essentially acting as though she were the party planner and caterer for this particular occasion. She likely had a to-do list a mile long, a schedule for everything from guest arrival to bread-making and then breaking. When she spies her sister doing absolutely nothing, by her estimation, she is not having it. No way would Mary's choice to sit like a stump on a log delay or interfere with Martha's carefully planned time-table. It probably comes as no surprise that Martha wasn't shy about letting her feelings known, shown in this charming exchange in Luke 10:40-42.

But Martha was distracted by all the preparations that had to be made. She came to him and asked, "Lord, don't you care that my sister has left me to do the work by myself? Tell her to help me!"

"Martha, Martha," the Lord answered, "you are worried and upset about many things, but few things are needed—or indeed only one. Mary has chosen what is better, and it will not be taken away from her."

If you're a Mary, keep it up! Your gaze is fixated in the right direction. If you're Martha, you should genuinely feel appreciated for all you do for others, but it's critical to keep the main thing the main thing.

I think Martha is sincerely trying to create a lovely, welcoming, five-star experience for Jesus, her house guest. She is serving in her own way.

The difference is she is serving in her own way. That's not a typo. While Mary is planted so that she hears every word coming from Jesus' mouth, Martha can hear none of them. She's in her own world doing what she has determined should be done on the time table she has concocted all on her own.

Her schedule, much like mine on the interstate is very ego-centric. It's all about us. And when things interfere, the delays are a nuisance because we're moving so fast we can't stop long enough to see them as opportunities.

God has called us all to be responsible, helpful servants. But He has also called us to be His children. He has called us to be His. As such, our time and energy should be oriented around things of His leading and calling. When we get so busy and frenetic doing all the good things we think we should do, we work our way out of ear shot and end up having to guess, assume and hope that we're on the right track.

In both of these stories (that of the disciples and the children and that of Mary and Martha), there is a consistent theme that rises from each delay. The world, our lives and the people in it do not revolve around our own timetables. What appears to be late to us could be ideal or even early according to God's purposes. The challenge to us all is to buy in to His agenda and relinquish our own. It's up to us to hand over the reigns of our lives to the one who has been writing our story all along. Today, maybe instead of checking your phone for the time of your next appointment, you check out the people around you and their needs. Perhaps instead of wrestling your priorities to the top of the list, you spend some time in the Word, considering God's priorities.

You and I will never understand the workings of God, much less His timing. What we can understand, though, is that He's never late. So whether you're stuck in traffic, waiting for an appointment or waiting for a miracle, let your wait time be one of hopeful expectation and earnest intention.

∂ß

DAILY DARE

1. Take a look at your daily schedule. Does it in any way revolve around someone other than yourself?

2. Think about the last time you were waiting for someone or something. What was your mood? How did you use the time in-between?

3. Challenge yourself to a day without agenda. Put away your phone, your schedule and even your watch. Pray for His leading, His timing and His patience throughout the day. At the end, write down what you experienced, how your day was different and give thanks for His perfect timing.

dare to

CELEBRATE THE JOURNEY

by G

DARE TO *CELEBRATE THE JOURNEY*

You prepare a table before me in the presence of my enemies;
You have anointed my head with oil; My cup overflows.

Psalm 23:5

It's always good to consider that, while attributes like consistency, discipline, hard work, commitment, loyalty, truth and persistence may not appear exciting, these are the very qualities that make the exciting possible. Think of the most fabulous things you've experienced— a wedding that was breath-taking, a party that was so elegant, a house beautifully furnished, art magnificently painted... Those things we appreciate and admire did not just happen; they were the result of the more mundane things we tend to gloss over. They are the result of disciplines that aren't exciting or elegant, but just plain hard work.

No great adventure happens without greater preparation. EVEN GOD PREPARES A TABLE FOR YOU. No incredible parties take place without incredible planning and commitment. No graduation day arrives without much revision and examination. No miraculous breakthroughs happen on the back of apathy. So when you're in the stages of preparation don't hold off the celebration. Get excited about the work that is helping you reach the place where you want to be. Be excited about the power of the preparation and be expectant as you stay disciplined.

When we delay our excitement, we can resent our journey. But when you have an understanding that what you do now will lead to where you want to be later, you see something to celebrate everyday.

So let's break that down into the day before you. If you are working on a project for your job, think ahead to all the things it can achieve—the strength it is building, the people you are meeting. If today looks like mundane care-taking of your family, think of the seeds you are sowing that will enable their future to flourish. Every part of the preparation is a new level of progress. Identify those areas we tend to look past and celebrate them now.

I am well-known for my obsession with lists. I have lists for everything. The lists are now the running joke in my family. If in doubt, go to the list! Yet those lists to me are just as important and speak even more profoundly of my love for those they involve. The list says I am preparing for others to be cared for when I am gone. I have thought ahead about what you may need. The list says I may not be here, but my heart is all here. The list speaks of a love that doesn't just show up at an event, but plans and prepares and nurtures for the things before, during and after. Today don't resent the list-making preparation. See it as seed-sowing and future-building.

Today, find joy in the simple things, because they are what make the spectacular days possible!

DAILY DARE

1. Do you find it difficult to celebrate the mundane? Is it easy to lose sight of the end-goal amongst the non-exciting daily task-list?

2. Break down your daily schedule. Can you tie each task, no matter how rote or mundane, to a bigger goal or celebration in the future? Is that staff meeting one step closer to your year-end goal? Is that practice you will be taking your child to and retrieving them from another step on the way to musical or athletic greatness? Or at least another mark on the "well-rounded" check list for future college or university? Train yourself to start seeing the bigger picture and celebrating it on the smallest of scales.

3. Schedule in celebration! Add in a coffee or ice cream break at the end of your day—or even in the middle! Intentionally weave in the excitement, appreciation and expectation and watch how your entire persona is lifted.

dare to

ROLL THE STONE AWAY

by ng

DARE TO *ROLL THE STONE AWAY*

Jesus, once more deeply moved, came to the tomb. It was a cave with a stone laid across the entrance. "Take away the stone," he said.

John 11:38-39

Three words can evoke a sense of anticipation, fear, worry, excitement, etc., more than just about any others...

Wait and see.

We get tests at a doctor's office and then...we wait and see.

We apply to a dream school or job and then...we wait and see.

We pray and then...we wait and see.

When the results are finally back or we get that letter in the mail from a school or business, as eager as we have been to know the status, it can seem nearly impossible to open the envelope, talk with the doctor and learn the answer to our prayers.

I can imagine Mary and Martha felt the same way following the death of their brother, Lazarus.

If you recall, Mary and Martha opened their home to Jesus. They were friends. And when Lazarus got sick, they reached out to their friend, Jesus. But Lazarus died before Jesus even reached their town.

When they saw Jesus approaching, Martha ran to Him.

"Lord," Martha said to Jesus, "if you had been here, my brother would not have died. But I know that even now God will give you whatever you ask." John 11:21-22

Soon, Mary followed suit...sort of.

When Mary reached the place where Jesus was and saw Him, she fell at His feet and said, "Lord, if you had been here, my brother would not have died." John 11:32

Notice the difference in the sisters' responses? Mary placed a period at the end of her statement. There was no expectation of anything else being done. She knew she had prayed and reached out to Jesus but her brother died anyway. That was all she could see.

Martha, on the other hand says something similar, with one huge caveat. Where as Mary thought the possibility of healing was over, Martha knew that with God, there was still a chance.

At the tomb where Lazarus lay, Jesus wept over the loss of His friend and then asked the by-standers to roll the stone away.

Can you imagine what they must have been thinking? Scripture shares that Lazarus had been dead for four days. Mary and Martha warned Jesus that the stench would be horrendous.

At the same time, to see the calm and compassion in Jesus' eyes, they must have had an inkling that a miracle could happen. As long as that stone was in place, that inkling could still be real for them. Maybe, just maybe there was still a chance.

Once the stone was moved, however, be it a miracle or a tragedy, they would have the answer. They would know the outcome. In a way, whatever was inside that tomb would signal the end of hoping. He would either be alive or be dead.

Despite the fear of whatever outcome they would soon see, the sisters did what Jesus asked and had the stone rolled away. Once the door was open, Jesus looked to His Father, prayed and commanded Lazarus to come out.

He did. And Jesus said to them, "Take off the grave clothes and let him go."

Their stone that rolled away led to a miracle. Your stone might too...or it might not. My stone might as well...or it might not. But we'll never know if we don't look.

What we do know is that God hears prayers. He hears yours. He knows what's on the other side of your stone. He knows what you will need to face whatever has been concealed and He is eager to equip you.

It's not a question or issue of bravery. Martha and Mary probably didn't feel brave at all when they obeyed Jesus' command. They didn't know what they would find. But they did know Jesus. It was their faith in Him that enabled them to open the tomb. It was the promise of His presence, strength, assurance and compassion that gave them the fortitude to find out the answer to their prayers.

So, when that letter comes or the doctor calls, have hope. Hope that, no matter the outcome, you will not go through it alone. The Savior who rolled His own stone away wants nothing more than for you to take a deep breath, lean in to Him and side-by-side discover what lies on the other side of yours.

$$\mathscr{db}$$

DAILY DARE

1. What is lying in wait behind your stone? What outcome are you desperately hoping to discover?

2. What is the source of your trepidation in learning the truth? What are you afraid you might find?

3. Think of the most pressing matter in your life at this moment. Has the anticipation of an outcome paralyzed you? If so, consider shifting the focus of your attention and prayers. Start seeking God's provision for whatever lies ahead.

dare to

CIRCLE THE PROMISE

by G

DARE TO *CIRCLE THE PROMISE*

And the Lord said to Joshua: "See! I have given Jericho into your hand,
its king, and the mighty men of valor. You shall march around the city, all you
men of war; you shall go all around the city once. This you shall do six days."

Joshua 6:2-3

When God had His people circle Jericho, it wasn't to tease them, but to teach them. Jericho was a problem, but one they had to surround before they could see the promise—that the walls would fall, and they would conquer the enemy; not by power, but through their patience and trust.

We all have those situations that intimidate us and seem too difficult to tackle. Maybe yours deserves a second look. Instead of seeing the walls and barriers before you, visualize His word. Don't focus on the problem; look for the promise. Save your shouting for when it's necessary. Use your waiting to wage a different kind of warfare; one of trust over stress. One where your peace is not dependent on instant results, but on an unchanging Savior.

No one likes to go around in circles. It's no fun seeing the same scenery over and over again. But at times God will have you circle a situation. It is not because He is teasing you or trying to punish you in any way. He is teaching you. Sometimes circling has more to do with things shifting around on your inside before change is evident around you.

Jericho could have fallen after the first lap, but that wouldn't have achieved the same results inside the children of Israel that seven times around did. God had them not only circle their problem, but also sleep outside its walls every night. They had seen it from every angle and imagined what lay within as they stood around it.

Jericho was so real to them but God was at work replacing that reality with a much greater one. He wanted them to circle those walls until they no longer saw a problem, but a promise that was theirs to possess. What is greater in your mind—the problem or the promise? What's more impressive—the unchanging word of God or the ever-changing difficulty and circumstances that have formed walls in your world? Where is your trust—in the structure or the Savior?

Maybe the reason for your extra lap is not because you can't see the walls, but because you can't see past them. Maybe you are going around again because, as you do, you can begin to replace what you see with a truth that is unseen—the words that conquer the walls, the promises that are greater than the problems.

Today, circle up and take another lap of your situation. This time, though, instead of panicking or doubting, hold your tongue, keep the peace and remind your heart over and over that you are not in this alone. God is more than able to provide, heal and overcome the situation. Determine to have a heart that is not fearful but faith-filled. Circle the promise, not the problem, and everything will begin to change from the inside out.

DAILY DARE

1. What are you making laps around today? Do you see your situation as a problem?

2. If you were to reframe where you are at this moment in terms of God's promises to you, what would that look like? For example, instead of: *These medical bills are piling up and I can't see any extra income coming in to take care of them.*

   Reframe to: *I am so fortunate to live in an area where I have access to health care and quality doctors to treat even the unexpected. I don't know where the money for these bills will come from, but God saw me through the illness and I will trust Him with this too.*

dare to be

ENOUGH

by ng

DARE TO BE *ENOUGH*

For I am the least of the apostles and do not even deserve to be called
an apostle, because I persecuted the church of God. But by the grace
of God I am what I am, and His grace to me was not without effect.
No, I worked harder than all of them—yet not I, but the grace of God
that was with me. By the grace of God, I am what I am.

1 Corinthians 15:10

I've learned some hard lessons in life. When it comes to relationships, my faith, my career and my family, I have made misstep after misstep. But every time I stumbled, I learned a new way to stand back up again, a little sturdier than before.

There is one lesson, one concept, one goal that has been harder to grasp than others. It's an idea that I know in my head to be true, but find it difficult to buy into within my heart. It's quite simple...just three little words...

I am enough.

Though I write it today with a period at the end, it is much more frequently a statement I turn into a question. It's hard for me to really feel I am adequate in a variety of capacities. Am I a good enough mom? A good enough wife? Friend? Follower of Christ?

Even while these questions tumble around in my head, I am fully aware that I'm not asking the right question. Why?

Because it's a moot point.

Because I already know the answer.

Am I good enough?

No. I'm not.

And you're not either.

That's not a dig. It's a statement of truth and freedom. Once we realize our own inadequacy, we can then be receptive to the one and only being whoever has been and ever will be enough...God. He is so adequate, in fact, that He created us to be incomplete without Him. The only way we will ever be enough for anyone, even for ourselves, is when we stop trying to be and instead fling ourselves into the open arms of Christ who was and is enough in every way.

As one who has waged this battle for years, I've discovered that I wasn't always looking in the right places or asking the right questions.

Somehow, I thought if I reached a certain position within the music industry and won this many awards, then I would finally be good enough as an artist.

I also thought if I could make every single event for my children and husband, make dinner every night, keep up with laundry, cleaning, etc., then I might feel as though my household contributions were enough.

I was wrong!

Truth is, it doesn't matter what I do or don't do. It doesn't matter what the external world thinks about who I am. What matters is Whose I am.

I am the daughter of the Savior and Creator of the world. I am covered in the redeeming blood of Christ. The Holy Spirit dwells within my heart. These are the things that define my adequacy. I am enough because He is enough.

That's pretty easy to write down or to say out loud. It's a lot harder to believe. So when self-doubt begins to creep in and I feel myself starting to overcompensate for areas in which I think I am inadequate, I go back to the source; to the words of the One who calls me His own. There, I read about grace. I can see mercy shown to people who are a lot like me—broken, unsure, tethered to the past.

And I see transformation. Perhaps none so profound as that of the Apostle Paul.

His very own words share his journey from persecutor to believer to apostle. He acknowledges how unlikely and nonsensical of a candidate he is to be God's mouthpiece. He who murdered Christians for their faith—now the greatest proclaimer of God's truth in history.

His resume didn't line up with that role. His history did not give him adequate training in love and mercy and Christ-like behaviors. His actions did not warrant forgiveness.

He was not enough.

But for grace...

And that's where it all comes down. It is the Grace of God that pines for us, sees us as we are and loves us. It is His grace that is sufficient.

It is enough. Therefore, no matter my self-doubt, mistakes or misgivings, I am enough.

When you look in the mirror, can you honestly repeat that phrase?

I am enough.

If not, I suggest a deep dive into the arms of grace. Your mirror reflects your face. But is is His grace that represents your heart.

No matter what.

We have all sinned and fallen short. But Jesus' sacrifice on the cross was more than enough to not just pick up the slack; but to overwhelm our very being to the point when we are no longer so pre-occupied with ourselves to even question adequacy or lack thereof. His desire is for us to live a life that is full; not one encumbered with doubt and feelings of worthlessness.

When we get to that point—the point at which we don't just say we are His; the point at which our lives become an irrefutable representation of Jesus Christ — our time and energy can be channeled away from ourselves and into the lives of others who need God's grace and love.

Grace is never predicated on our actions.

Mercy isn't rationed according to the strength of our faith.

Love itself did not die on a cross and rise again because of our adequacy or inadequacy. Whether we were enough to warrant such a sacrifice is immaterial.

It doesn't even start with us.

It is because of His love for you and for me that we are covered in the blood of Christ, free from shame and guilt.

Because He first loved you and me, we are enough; we are overflowing from an abundance that will never end.

Go back and take a look in the mirror one more time. Forget the questions... just repeat the truth:

I am more than enough. I am His. I am a child of unending grace, forgiveness and love. And because He is enough, so too am I.

DAILY DARE

1. What is dragging you into a pit of self-doubt and inadequacy?

2. If you were to look back on your life, do you notice any patterns of behavior linked to your sense of self-worth?

3. Do you dare to throw yourself head-long into the adequacy of His love? Pray today that His sufficiency overwhelms and undercuts your sense of self-doubt. Pray that His adequacy floods your senses to the point of overflow...to the point at which your life is no longer a "me" exercise, but an outward-facing, others-oriented display of His grace, mercy and love.

dare to

GO HOME

by *G*

DARE TO *GO HOME*

The righteous will flourish like a palm tree, they will grow like
a cedar of Lebanon; planted in the house of the Lord, they will flourish
in the courts of our God. They will still bear fruit in old age,
they will stay fresh and green, proclaiming, "The Lord is upright;
He is my Rock, and there is no wickedness in Him."

Psalm 92:13-15

So much of our lives are shaped by the place we call home. Whether your first was good or bad, a place filled with love or a place you wanted to leave, its effect on you is undeniable. Every heart, no matter its experience, longs to find that place that is "home sweet home." The heart longs to belong, to have a place amongst all the unfamiliar, a place that is known, a place that's consistent.

If you have ever been amongst homelessness, you know first-hand that that lifestyle is not what your Heavenly Father had in mind for anyone. Living in a place of detachment and vulnerability, unsettled and uprooted is pretty much the opposite of what God wants for our lives.

Just as much as we would want to help those who find themselves physically homeless, we also need to have a heart to help and eyes to see the spiritually homeless. This is an ever-increasing epidemic that demands attention and compassion to address the fact that as God's children, we are not designed to live as nomads. We are destined to be planted. In that planting resides the key to future flourishing. Many are looking for fruit that can only be found when they finally come home.

Of course, homelessness isn't the only situation in which one could find oneself without a home. Dreamers without roots become drifters and talent without residency becomes a traveling road show. Performance replaces permanence and spectators take the place God had intended for co-workers and supporters.

God, in His wisdom, designed your life and mine to be an adventure. But He also intended for you to find the strength that comes when every adventure is anchored in Him. He is so intent on acquiring your love and you fulfilling your purpose, He has not only called you; He wants to plant you. He doesn't just say believe; He also wants you to belong.

For many, the concept of being planted somehow is viewed as detrimental to their future. Home becomes a place they can only see as chores and tasks. They have developed a modified form of home-sickness. They are sick of the work that is necessary to build a home and the lessons one must learn to maintain it. So they pack up their lives and trade in roots for fewer responsibilities and far less accountability. However, when restlessness is allowed to choose our direction, we must be aware that whatever escape we may find, it is temporary—not a permanent abode.

Let's not forget the incredible gift of having a home—a place that builds you up and unites you with people that shape and help you grow. A community that contributes alongside and with you... An address for the lost, weary and hurting to come and unpack their lives...

Let's have such passion for planting that it leads to outrageous flourishing. Let's not resent the homework, but remember in Whose house we are honored to serve. His is the model home which I try to emulate in my own household. I love being a small part of something so much greater. Whatever your story or wherever this finds you. God is always calling you to Himself and to His house saying, "Welcome Home."

db

DAILY DARE

1. Describe the home you grew up in. What was wonderful? Terrible? What taught you and what defeated you?

2. Examine your current home situation. Does it build you up? Is it a place of warmth and hospitality towards others? Be honest!

3. Determine the kind of home you want to create. Write down what is important to you and start putting in the work to make home sweet home a dream come true.

dare to be

CLEAN

by ng

DARE TO BE *CLEAN*

"Come now, and let us reason together," Says the Lord,
"Though your sins are like scarlet, they shall be as white as snow;
though they are red like crimson they shall be as wool."

Isaiah 1:18 (NKJV)

Have you ever stained something you knew was going to be a lost cause? For instance, I once knew someone who washed all of her husband's good work shirts along with his good work ink pen. You can imagine how that played out. He got new work shirts for his birthday!

Some stains are just in too deep. They are beyond repair.

Your stains are not that way. Neither are mine. Nor anyone else's. There is no aspect of us that is too dirty or too soiled to be washed clean.

On my album, *Be One,* one of the songs came to me in one of the most clearly God-inspired moments of my life. While I've never heard His voice audibly speak to me, it was so evident that His hand was guiding my pen.

The song came after a conversation I had with a friend earlier that very day. She had been carrying a secret.

For years.

So convinced was she of the shame and filth that she associated with an abuse she suffered in childhood, she could barely get the words out. All I could do was listen. Then we prayed, cried and read Scripture together.

When she left, I started thinking about how many people must feel that their lives bear an indelible stain. That something that had been done to them or they had done to another had simply pierced too deep and could never be completely healed.

I couldn't help but think that they could be walking around and smiling and worshiping and going to church, but inside have this open wound. This idea of, "I'm too dirty," struck me. I couldn't shake it and I literally started singing, "There's nothing too dirty, that You can't make worthy."

I've been waging a war on human trafficking for over ten years. I remember with such clarity a church I was at where the pastor asked me not to make mention of it. It was a "family night" and that topic was too dirty to include.

That has stayed with me forever, compelling me to keep telling the truth. The church is a place where we should be able to talk about everything in safety and feel comforted and comfortable. Those voices that label some topics as taboo are the ones contriving this thing of "religion" which isn't representative of Christ at all.

To be a Christian—Christ-like—requires a relationship and a transformation. That transformation is one from dirty to clean.

Thus, when we have things in our past or we see things in the world that are painful and dirty and make us uncomfortable, the first place we should take them is to the One who makes all things clean.

Today, I dare you to believe that you are clean—to believe that nothing from your yesterday can stain your today or tomorrow. There is nothing you could bring to Christ that is off-limits. He is the one who makes the unworthy worthy, the unloved loved and the unclean whiter than snow.

DAILY DARE

1. What is your stain? Is there something in your past you feel is leaving a mark on your heart that will never come out?

2. Do you find yourself judging the situations and circumstances of others? Of trying to push some topics out the door because they're not "family-friendly?"

3. Pray to be convicted of your stains and to be convinced that He has made you clean. And pray to be a safe place for others to bring their wounds and stains. Pray for a heart and spirit as clean as the One who created them.

dare to

PROCESS THE PAIN

by G

DARE TO *PROCESS THE PAIN*

Fixing our eyes on Jesus, the pioneer and perfecter of faith.
For the joy set before Him, He endured the cross, scorning its shame,
and sat down at the right hand of the throne of God.

Hebrews 12:2

What ever you focus on will become the reality of your life. It's a well-known concept and a solid observation. The more attention we give something and the more we feed it, the greater are the odds that it will grow. The inverse is also true. Whatever we neglect or starve, the weaker it becomes. Where we place our focus, concentration and meditation is crucial! This can be difficult to manage, particularly in times of pain, the power of which lies in its ability to demand attention. Pain is like a clarion call to each part of your life, screaming, "Look at me, tend to me, adjust around me!" While you should always confront and deal with your pain, it doesn't necessarily deserve center stage.

On the other hand, while our pain shouldn't monopolize our lives, it's important to recognize that it is also a part of the progress we seek.

You can't grow without stretching. You can't get stronger without building more stamina. You can't birth something without enduring labor. Our understanding of the role of the pain we experience comes down to perspective. We can label pain as an enemy to combat or as a training partner; perhaps even a friend.

Pain intrinsically has the ability to hurt, and also, the capacity to help. The paradigm through which we monitor pain produces different outcomes depending on the angle and focus we assume. Before pain has the chance to speak, it's up to us to determine how much stage time it receives.

For example, if you have had the awkward, even uncomfortable, encounter of listening to a woman's labor story, it will no doubt involve several statements of pain. Yet they will be told from a perspective of joy as that pain was what helped bring forth the baby. The storyteller sits lovingly, holding the baby who has stolen the spotlight, erased memories of the birthing pains and is now enjoying the attention of everyone in the room.

Jesus and His journey to the cross beautifully illustrates this. The cross was the most agonizing death imaginable. The pain was unbearable, but it did not consume Jesus' full attention. Christ considered the cross "the joy set before Him," because it was the conduit by which He would one day commune with you and with me. Rather than the nails, the beatings, the thorns, we who had not even been born were in His spotlight, center stage. Pain delivered a cameo, but it was most certainly not a scene stealer—nor should it be.When it comes down to it, no one really enjoys pain. However, I am learning more and more to listen to it and allow its message to help me in my understanding.

Today, when pain comes knocking, determine not to be defeated. Look to the front, the back and in every other direction around you for clues on processing your pain in a way that is healthy, deliberate and reflective of the heart of Christ. Don't ignore it; rather, pay attention to the symptoms. Spend your energy finding a cure; not dwelling on the source.

db

DAILY DARE

1. What pain has you in its grip at the moment? Can you identify any impact on your life from this particular pain?

2. Start to reframe your pain. Focus on what potentially positive outcomes could emanate and choose to spend your energy traveling in that direction.

3. Revisit a pain from the past that left you feeling defeated and depleted. In retrospect, what did you learn from that experience? How can you apply those lessons today?

dare to

BELIEVE YOUR OUTCOME DOESN'T DETERMINE HIS GOODNESS

by ng

DARE TO *BELIEVE YOUR OUTCOME DOESN'T DETERMINE HIS GOODNESS*

"Abba, Father," he said, "everything is possible for you.
Take this cup from me. Yet not what I will, but what you will."

Mark 14:36

JESUS more than anything.

I love that phrase. There's a poetic beauty and cadence to the simple notion that above all else, there is Jesus. It's a lovely idea and a powerful prayer.

"Oh Jesus, help us seek Your face before we seek Your hand. Help us love You because of WHO YOU ARE, not because of what you can do for us."

Such a noble sentiment and honorable pursuit! Such a bold, brave mindset to adopt!

Such a difficult destination for many of us to reach. It's much easier to say this prayer than it is to actually live it, breathe it or trust it.

Two years ago, I recorded a song about this very thing, called, "More Than Anything." The lyrics were inspired by the story of a woman battling a horrific cancer. While the disease ravaged her body, her heart's cry was, "I know you can heal me Lord, but even if you choose not to in this life, help me want the Healer, more than the healing."

I'll never forget being in the studio, recording the song, thinking of so many people who were facing the unthinkable. I prayed that the words would become a lifeline; that "JESUS more than anything" could become a mantra for everyone out there facing the impossible.

Fast-forward a couple of years. It was in the middle of August. My record company came to me and said they wanted to make that song my new release to radio. "Awesome," I thought. And I began to pray again that it would push people towards the only answer: JESUS.

Fast-forward just one month. It was in the middle of September.

And I was diagnosed with cancer.

I was set to sing this song for a huge radio conference the same week of my diagnosis, and as I was rehearsing, I got to the lyrics of the chorus: help me want the Healer, more than the healing...I couldn't get the words out.

"No!" I screamed in my mind. "No! No! No!" This song was for someone else's story. But God knew back in 2015 when I recorded it that He was going to help me learn to live it two years later.

And so, I walked out on that stage and sang the song. I felt like such a fraud, because honestly, I just wanted the healing. But I so tangibly and sincerely felt Him say, "Get your mind off your circumstances and focus your eyes on ME. Stop thinking of all that you need me to do for you. Start thinking about WHO I AM. Write it down, say it out loud. Do it continually and it will take root."

So I did.

You are my Savior.

You are my Father.

You are my Healer.

You are my Protector.

You are my Provider.

You are faithful.

You are kind.

You are good.

You are sovereign.

Your love knows no end.

His truth brings silence to the noise. We serve a God whose ways are higher than our own.

Sometimes we undergo loss and tragedy that make no sense. We can't find rationale. I don't understand those losses anymore than you do. There are some questions that are just too big. But I do know that we can all make one small change that may set in motion one of the most heart-freeing, eye-opening shifts in our lives. Rather than seeking our own outcomes; our desires and hopes; our cures or remedies, let us instead seek His goodness, His face, His heart.

Just like Jesus in the Garden of Gethsemane, we must lay down our will for His. Jesus asked for the cup to be taken from Him. But He knew, regardless of the outcome, that God's will would prevail and it would be a testament to His goodness.

No matter what, He still had a good Father.

So do you.

So do I.

Our outcomes do not determine His goodness. As I focused on Him and Him alone, I began to experience His peace that completely surpasses understanding. I'm talking about a calm in the depth of my soul that doesn't even make sense. I actually felt His nearness in a way I had never experienced before. I encountered His presence in a way I never knew possible.

Sometimes it takes walking through the valley of the shadow of death to get us there.

His favor often comes in the package of suffering and hardship. He uses our uncertainties, the unknowns, the devastations to reveal His character—personal, always reaching, always pursuing us to dive deeper into His love. In order to go higher, we must go deeper.

No matter what we are in the middle of, God is already HERE. And no matter what lies ahead, God is already THERE. His goodness is unwavering no matter what. It's up to us to decide to claim it, regardless of our outcome; to pursue Healer above the heaing.

Like my song says:

Help me want the Healer

more than the healing.

Help me want the Savior

more than the saving.

Help me want the Giver

more than the giving.

Help me want you JESUS

more than anything.

JESUS more than anything.

DAILY DARE

1. Is there something in your life right now with an uncertain outcome? How does that make you feel?

2. Start keeping a prayer journal. Take notes about your conversations with God. Do this for a few weeks then review it. Note any patterns you observe. Does the bulk of your prayer time revolve around you, your hardships or desires? How much time do you spend talking to Him about Him? How much time do you spend listening?

3. If you were to make this the day that you put Jesus above everything, what would that look like? What would look and be different about your life? What are you waiting for?

FOR MORE RESOURCES
by Natalie Grant & Charlotte Gambill please visit:

daretobe.com
instagram/@daretobeevent
facebook.com/daretobeevent

For Dare To Be apparel please visit:
daretobe.com

OTHER RESOURCES BY NATALIE GRANT:
nataliegrant.com

FINDING YOUR VOICE *book*
BE ONE *album*
HURRICANE *album*
GLIMMER GIRLS BOOK SERIES *books for tween girls*

OTHER BOOKS BY CHARLOTTE GAMBILL:
charlottegambill.com

MIRACLE IN THE MIDDLE
TURNAROUND GOD
NOW WHAT?
IN HER SHOES

ABOUT THE AUTHORS

NATALIE GRANT

Seven-time Grammy nominated and multi Dove Award winner, Natalie Grant, has become an iconic name in Christian music, using her platform to continually point people to the love, hope and restorative power of Jesus Christ for nearly two decades.

In addition to her music, Natalie has authored several books, and is also known for her philanthropic work. She is co-founder of Hope For Justice International; an organization that rescues and restores victims of human trafficking, with offices in 11 countries across 4 continents. Natalie resides in Nashville, TN with her husband, music producer Bernie Herms, and their three daughters - Gracie, Bella and Sadie.

nataliegrant.com

instagram @nataliegrant

facebook.com/nataliegrantmusic

CHARLOTTE GAMBILL

International speaker and author, Charlotte Gambill, is best known for her practical and passionate application of Gods Word. She speaks at conferences across the world and her passion is to build the local church, to see people reach their full potential, and to develop and strengthen church leadership. She and her husband, Steve Gambill, pastor LIFE Church, UK; a growing ministry with 2 campuses in England, and additional campuses in Warsaw, Poland and Belfast, Ireland. Together they have two children, Hope Cherish and Noah Brave.

charlottegambill.com

instagram @charlgambill

facebook.com/charlgambill

lifechurchhome.com